A CATHOLIC RESPONSE TO THE JEHOVAH'S WITNESSES

Revised Edition

Jennifer Moorcroft

Copyright © 2024 by Jennifer Moorcroft.

ISBN: 979-8-89465-094-4 (sc)
ISBN: 979-8-89465-095-1 (e)

All rights reserved. No part of this publication may be reproduced, distributed, or transmitted in any form or by any means, including photocopying, recording, or other electronic or mechanical methods, without the prior written permission of the author, except in the case of brief quotations embodied in critical reviews and certain other noncommercial uses permitted by copyright law.

Printed in the United States of America.

Integrity Publishing
39343 Harbor Hills Blvd Lady Lake,
FL 32159

www.integrity-publishing.com

TABLE OF CONTENTS

Introduction v

PART 1 – What Watchtower Teaching Is Based On
Chapter 1:   A Jehovah's Witness On Your Doorstep 3
Chapter 2:   Bible Only Christians? 7
Chapter 3:   Using The Church Fathers 27
Chapter 4:   Is The Catholic Church Pagan? 32

PART 2 – Catholic Doctrines Under Fire
Chapter 5:   The Triune God, Father, Son and
             Holy Spirit 41
Chapter 6:   Jehovah God 58
Chapter 7:   Jesus Christ, Son of God 63
Chapter 8:   The Holy Spirit 89
Chapter 9:   Cross or Torture Stake 95
Chapter 10: The Ransom Sacrifice of Jesus 102

PART 3 – Watchtower Teachings
Chapter 11: The Immortality of the Soul 109
Chapter 12: Hell 118
Chapter 13: The Resurrection 128
Chapter 14: The 144,000 142
Chapter 15: Heaven 150

Chapter 16: 1914 and All That 154
Chapter 17: Armageddon 166
Chapter 18: Paradise Earth 169
Chapter 19: Kingdom of Heaven. 183

PART 4 – Inside The Organisation
Chapter 20: Becoming a Jehovah's Witness. 189
Chapter 21: Leaving the Watchtower. 201
Chapter 22: Not of this World. 204
Chapter 23: Disfellowshipping 208
Chapter 24: The Watchtower and War 213
Chapter 25: Blood Transfusions 220

PART 5 – Catholic Practices Under Fire
Chapter 26: Birthdays, Christmas and Easter 227
Chapter 27: Celebrating Mary and the Saints 232
Chapter 28: The Pope and Priests 238
Conclusion 243
Appendix 1 245
Appendix 2 247
Bibliography 257

INTRODUCTION

Over the years my husband and I have received many visits from the Jehovah's Witnesses, mostly by being given a leaflet, but we have also invited them in to discuss their religious beliefs. Listening to them, I can understand how their teachings can have a certain persuasiveness. Their conviction of the rightness of their teachings, their promise of paradise on earth, combined with the underlying threat that to reject those teachings is to lose a future happiness and suffer destruction, can draw people to accept those teachings.

The Jehovah's Witnesses stress that there are many ex-Catholics in their organisation, and some we have spoken to have said they were ex-Catholics. (It is also true that many Jehovah's Witnesses have left the organisation and have come into the Catholic Church). But it is for those Catholics, especially, that this handbook is written. Seeing many Catholics leave the Faith for the Witnesses, I wanted to enable them, before they make a final decision, to have a tool to help them assess dispassionately the truth or falsehood of the Watchtower organisation while they still have the ability to think for themselves. For those who want to leave the Jehovah's Witnesses, perhaps it will be helpful to have material to help them in this journey.

What qualifications do I have for this task? To begin with, I am a convert to the Catholic Faith - over sixty years ago now - although not from the Watchtower. While I was drawing closer to the Church I deliberately read both Catholic and anti- or –non-Catholic books, so that I could see the issues from both sides. Since then, I haven't stopped studying and deepening my Catholic Faith, and with each encounter with Jehovah's Witnesses, I have turned to the Scriptures and to the Church's teachings to compare the two. I have found there truths that truly satisfy, and in the light of which the Watchtower teachings are shown up in all their inadequacy and their departure from orthodox Christianity.

What I hope this handbook will do is give Catholics a good resource to counter Watchtower teachings, and to assure them of the sound base on which their own faith rests.

PART 1
WHAT WATCHTOWER TEACHING IS BASED ON

This section deals with what happens when Jehovah's Witnesses knock at your door. Should you send them away or invite them in? They come as Bible-believing Christians. Do you know the Scriptures well enough to feel confident of responding to them adequately? Do you feel confident enough of your Faith to give a good response to those who would challenge it?

CHAPTER 1

A JEHOVAH'S WITNESS ON YOUR DOORSTEP

The doorbell rings and two Jehovah's Witnesses are on your doorstep. How do you react? The best advice is not to invite them in or to accept their literature. However, if this is what you decide to do, do it with graciousness. Witnesses have been taught that other Christians – especially Catholics! – are in the devil's organisation, so to find a courteous Catholic is not what they expect. They expect opposition, and even revel in it, as it reinforces their belief that they are being persecuted for their faith, so it is not necessary to give them the excuse to feel so.

A courteous encounter on a doorstep can leave a lasting impression. One convert described how, as a child, she went along with her mother 'pioneering', as doorstep evangelising is called. The door was opened by a lady wearing a large cross and a lovely smile, who declined to speak to them, but promised to pray for them. The child's mother yanked her away, muttering that they didn't want her prayers. The memory, though, of that loving encounter stayed with her and eventually she came home to the Catholic Church.

What happens if, instead, you invite them in or engage in a discussion on your doorstep? The Witnesses will probably begin by asking you what you think of the state of the world, or point you to a passage of Scripture that seems to describe its dire straits. You may probably agree with them that the world isn't in a very good state – one could hardly say anything else! My response is then to add that with faith in the Resurrection of Jesus I know God has the world in his care and his purposes will prevail. The Witnesses' aim is to latch on to some complaint, some dissatisfaction with the state of the world, or something in your own life or with your Church, so that they can then present you with the prospect of their 'hope for the future' – paradise earth, a warm and welcoming community at the 'Kingdom Hall', the assurance that you will have 'the truth'. Don't let them drag you into pessimism. Ours is a Resurrection faith.

They could ask you whether you would like to live forever in a world where all the evils of our present world no longer exist. Say no! – Your hope is to live eternally with God in heaven, to see him 'face to face' (Revelation 22:4). To say that you don't want to live in a paradise earth will probably disconcert them, but will also give them the opportunity to talk about their hope of paradise earth. This is one of their main doctrines, and we will discuss this in a later chapter.

If you have invited them into your home, they will then open their Bibles and invite you to take out your Bible so that they can share some 'Bible Truths' with you. At this point you might well regret inviting them in, because you may not feel at home enough with the Bible to feel happy about this; I will discuss this in the next chapter. You may not even have a Bible! However, don't worry; one Witness said that the hardest people to convert are Catholics who may not be at home with the Bible, but nevertheless have a love of God, even though they may not be able to argue their belief from the Scriptures. Living in union the Father, through Jesus Christ, in the love of the Holy Spirit, is the greatest 'armour' we have against Watchtower teachings.

Indoctrination

Anyone who has encountered the Jehovah's Witnesses will know how well indoctrinated in Watchtower teachings they are. They are so well trained in how to present their teachings that it seems very difficult to counter them. In their training meetings they are taught how to evade questions, change the subject, ignore what one says; how to stonewall if what you are saying falls outside what they have been taught. This is deliberate. Because they are taught that any interpretation that contradicts what the Watchtower teaches comes from the Devil's organisation, from 'apostates', they must not engage in discussion about it or take it on board.

It can seem that they are so well indoctrinated in Watchtower teachings that it is unlikely that they will be converted, at least immediately. However, appearances can be deceptive. Reading the conversion stories of those who have left the Witnesses it is striking how often, once they start to become disillusioned with the Watchtower organisation and its teachings, they can continue proselytising for some time, teaching others the doctrines they no longer believe in themselves. So you never know whether something you say of your own Catholic faith will pierce their armour and start them on their journey home to the Church, or at least out of the Watchtower Society. So remember to keep them in your prayer, for it is only the light of the Holy Spirit which can penetrate their hearts and minds and give them the courage to break away from the Watchtower organisation.

You will notice that I speak more of the Watchtower Society than of the Jehovah's Witnesses. This was the recommendation of another Catholic writing about the Jehovah's Witnesses, because when speaking to a Jehovah's Witness it will help put some distance between the Witness sitting in front of you, and the organisation to which they belong, and whose teachings you are opposing. You are not opposing the person but the teachings they are promulgating.

said that the hardest people to convert are Catholics who may not be at home with the Bible, but nevertheless have a love of God, even though they may not be able to argue their belief from the Scriptures. Living in union the Father, through Jesus Christ, in the love of the Holy Spirit, is the greatest 'armour' we have against Watchtower teachings.

Indoctrination

Anyone who has encountered the Jehovah's Witnesses will know how well indoctrinated in Watchtower teachings they are. They are so well trained in how to present their teachings that it seems very difficult to counter them. In their training meetings they are taught how to evade questions, change the subject, ignore what one says; how to stonewall if what you are saying falls outside what they have been taught. This is deliberate. Because they are taught that any interpretation that contradicts what the Watchtower teaches comes from the Devil's organisation, from 'apostates', they must not engage in discussion about it or take it on board.

It can seem that they are so well indoctrinated in Watchtower teachings that it is unlikely that they will be converted, at least immediately. However, appearances can be deceptive. Reading the conversion stories of those who have left the Witnesses it is striking how often, once they start to become disillusioned with the Watchtower organisation and its teachings, they can continue proselytising for some time, teaching others the doctrines they no longer believe in themselves. So you never know whether something you say of your own Catholic faith will pierce their armour and start them on their journey home to the Church, or at least out of the Watchtower Society. So remember to keep them in your prayer, for it is only the light of the Holy Spirit which can penetrate their hearts and minds and give them the courage to break away from the Watchtower organisation.

You will notice that I speak more of the Watchtower Society than of the Jehovah's Witnesses. This was the recommendation of another Catholic writing about the Jehovah's Witnesses, because when speaking to a Jehovah's Witness it will help put some distance between the Witness sitting in front of you, and the organisation to which they belong, and whose teachings you are opposing. You are not opposing the person but the teachings they are promulgating.

CHAPTER 2

BIBLE ONLY CHRISTIANS?

When the Jehovah's Witnesses come calling, they come armed with a Bible and declare themselves 'Bible alone' believers and are taught by their organisation that it alone interprets it correctly. A Catholic can feel at a disadvantage because the Jehovah's Witnesses give the impression that they know the Bible well and the Catholic might feel that he does not. The Watchtower interpretation can seem persuasive and there is a settled belief within the Watchtower that orthodox Christian beliefs are not based on the Scriptures; that Catholic teaching, above all, is wrong and has falsified the Scriptures. However, there are a great many passages that they completely ignore if they conflict with its teachings.

One of the problems a Catholic has when meeting the Jehovah's Witnesses – or sometimes with a non-Catholic Christian, come to that - is that the other person seems to have a much deeper knowledge of the Bible than the Catholic has. One reason is that many Catholics do not read the Bible very much as part of their personal prayer life, although we are strongly encouraged to do so, and it really should be an integral part of our Catholic life. Another reason is that the Catholic Church understands the Scriptures in a very different way from the Watchtower, and often, also, with non-Catholic denominations. Although I will be quoting a great deal of Scripture in later chapters, the Church does not have a 'chapter and verse' approach to the Scriptures. A Catholic should not be too ashamed that they do not know chapter and verse of the Scriptures as well as the Witnesses seem to do. However, they use only a small fraction of the Scriptures in their teachings, which is why they have no answer when confronted with a text with which they are unfamiliar and is not used by The Watchtower.

The Watchtower interprets the Scriptures in such a totally different way not only to the Catholic Church, but also to many of the mainstream Christian denominations, that discussing with Witnesses is like running on parallel lines that never meet. One can be fully conversant with a passage, and yet be completely thrown when confronted with a Watchtower interpretation.

Another problem is that the Watchtower will sometimes put a literal interpretation on a passage, such as interpreting the number of 144,000 in the book of Revelation literally, and yet totally ignore that the 144,000 are from the twelve tribes of Israel, in the very same verse! At other times it takes a highly original slant when the passage conflicts with its beliefs. For example, Jesus' parable of Dives and Lazarus, which supports the belief of life after death, becomes, in the Watchtower's eyes, a parable of the corruption of Christendom in the person of the rich man.

The Church lives the Scriptures

However, we Catholics are in fact imbued with the Scriptures when we go to Mass and take part in the sacraments and the liturgy of the Church. The Church's liturgy, her sacraments, her practice and her devotions, her prayer and worship, are saturated with the Scriptures. The Church is living the Scriptures in the whole of her being, so when a Catholic attends Mass, for example, he is imbibing a great deal of Scripture. We are encouraged to ponder the Scriptures that are read during the Liturgy of the Word and make them our own, especially when recent reforms to the liturgy are designed to help us in that. Even if we are unable to go to daily Mass, we are encouraged to follow the readings of the day, and there are many aids to understanding the readings; in this way we are praying the Scriptures with the Church in her liturgy. Over the yearly cycle of the liturgy we will be reading extracts from all the books of the Bible. Further, as we shall see, the Church was living the faith for several centuries before she set down what Scriptures defined that faith.

It does mean, though, that when discussing the Scriptures with a Witness, we may have to use texts in a literal way to counteract their arguments, when the Church's understanding has a much more profound approach.

How we got the Bible

As a Catholic you could point out to the Witnesses that the Bible they profess to revere and follow has actually been given to them by a Church that they consider is apostate and that has abandoned the pure teaching of the apostles. One Witness to whom I pointed this out could reply only that the Church did sometimes get things right! So how did we get the Bible?

From the very beginning, the four Gospels were given a very special place in the Church's devotion. The letters of St Paul were widely circulated, and Paul himself asks that they be passed on to the other churches (cf. Colossians 4:16). However, although there gradually came to be a consensus as to which writings were accepted as inspired, there was no generally accepted canon of the New Testament, and local churches had access to different writings and differing opinions as to what should be read in their liturgies. In A.D. 367 Saint Athanasius attested to the New Testament we have now, but it was only in the year 387 that Pope St Damasus promulgated the canon of Scriptures, a process that began with the Synod of Rome in 380, the Councils of Hippo and Carthage in 393 and 397, and was completed in A.D. 417. Before that, there were several lists of what books people felt could be included, and also excluded. For some time 2 Peter and 2 and 3 John were excluded, as well as Hebrews, Jude, Philemon and Revelation. Included could be the 1st Letter of St Clement to the Corinthians, the Epistle of Barnabus, the Shepherd of Hermas and the Didache, for example.

Why did the Church reject some writings and accept others? The criterion was that they should have been written by the first apostles or by those who had direct access to those who were eyewitness to the events of Christ's life, death and resurrection (cf. Luke 1:1-3). The writings that were accepted were those that were approved for reading within the context of the Liturgy. Of course, orthodox writings that were not included within this canon were not suppressed or destroyed, as some assert, but those that were consonant with the orthodox Christian faith are treasured and read as part of the rich inheritance of the Church.[1]

---

[1] As well as the writings of the Fathers of the Church, there were also the Apocryphal Gospels, as distinct from the heretical, Gnostic writings.

The content of Faith came before the Scriptures

The Church, therefore, had been living and teaching the Faith for nearly four hundred years before she affirmed definitively which writings were inspired by God and reflected the Church's teaching, and not the other way round. The Church can never teach or believe anything that is against Scripture, but in the Catholic Church we have both Scripture and Tradition (cf. 2 Thessalonians 2:15, 2 Corinthians 11:2); both the written word of the Scriptures and the oral tradition that has been handed down from the apostles.

How, then, does the Watchtower accept the authority of the Church when she tells it what books of the Bible are divinely inspired, but denies the doctrines and practices which the Church had already defined? For example, the Council of Nicea in A.D. 324 fixed the date of Easter, so the early Church was also already celebrating Easter before the Canon of the New Testament was fixed, but the Watchtower does not accept the celebration of Easter. The Church that gave us the Bible was the one that some sixty years earlier had formulated the Creed that affirmed that Jesus Christ was 'true God from true God, begotten not made, one in essence with the Father, God from God, Light from Light', teachings rejected by the Watchtower Society. The stipulation was made, when formulating the Creed, that there should not be anything in it that contradicts the books of the New Testament, so it was considered that these beliefs were truly consonant with the Scriptures.

How, then, can the Watchtower teachings be confronted? First, let us examine their claim that they are 'Bible Alone Christians'.

Bible alone?

The Jehovah's Witnesses say that their teachings are based solely on the Bible, but is this true? According to Charles Taze Russell, the founder of the Jehovah's Witnesses, they could do without the Bible if they had only the writings of the Watchtower Society, and on the other hand, could be in 'darkness' if they had only the Bible. This is correct, because the Watchtower teachings interpret the Scriptures in such an idiosyncratic way that no-one could independently glean their teachings from the Scriptures without Watchtower writings. Charles Taze Russell wrote:

> Not only do we find that people cannot see the divine in studying the Bible by itself, but we see, also, that if anyone lays the 'Scripture Studies' aside, even after he has used them, after he has become familiar with them, after he has read them for ten years – if he then lays them aside and ignores them and goes to the Bible alone, though he has understood his Bible for ten years, our experience shows that within two years he goes into darkness. On the other hand, if he had merely read the 'Scripture Studies' with their references and had not read a page of the Bible as such, he would be in the light at the end of two years, because he would have the light of the Scriptures.
> *The Watchtower 15/9/1910,* p. 298

The positive promise in this, of course, is that once they do lay aside Watchtower publications and read the Scriptures for themselves, they will understand how the Watchtower distorts the Scriptures.

No Bible without Watchtower interpretation

Russell's assertion that the Bible cannot be understood without Watchtower interpretation is something that is still the rule within the organisation, even though it no longer draws on his writings. The Watchtower certainly puts itself forward as the only true interpreter of the Scriptures:

> It should be expected that the Lord would have a means of communication to his people on earth, and he has clearly shown that the magazine called The Watchtower is used for that purpose.
> *Yearbook of Jehovah's Witnesses 1930,* p. 85

> Only this organisation functions for Jehovah's purpose and to his praise. To it alone God's Sacred Word, the Bible, is not a sealed book.
> *The Watchtower 1/7/1973,* p. 402

Further, The Watchtower does not consider that what it says is only its interpretation but is what the Bible is actually saying:

> All who want to understand the Bible appreciate that the 'greatly diversified wisdom of God' can become known only through Jehovah's channel of communication, the faithful and discreet slave.
> *The Watchtower 10/1/1994,* p. 8

Who is doing the interpretation?

Who is 'the faithful and discreet slave' who is the only one to give a true understanding of the Scriptures? – at one time this was the 'anointed class of the 144,000 but was later limited to the Board of Directors of the Watchtower Bible and Tract Society. William Cetnar, who worked in the editorial department of the Watchtower Headquarters for several years, reported a revealing statement of President Franz Knorr (President of the Watchtower at the time) in 1952, when the brothers in the editorial department had argued over a doctrinal matter. 'Brothers, you can argue all you want about it, but when it gets off the sixth floor *it is the truth*.'[2] (The sixth floor was where the printing presses were). In other words, there might be differences of opinion among the Directors, but once material was printed it became the truth which all had to accept. Knorr admitted in a court statement that the Board of Directors consider doctrinal statements and express their opinions but could say only that 'after the matter is published there is agreement'. According to Raymond Franz,[3] decisions were at that time made by the President, Nathan Knorr, Fred Franz and Karl Adams.

During one visit to me, a Jehovah's Witness was proud of the fact that they did not know the names of the Board of Directors who publish their magazines week by week, and tell them what they have to study and what they have to believe. In fact, after the time of Judge Rutherford, who did write books which appeared under his name, no

---

[2] Edmond Gruss, *We Left the Jehovah's Witnesses,* (Phillipsburg New Jersey, Presbyterian and Reformed Publishing Co., 1974), p. 78.

[3] Raymond Franz, *Crisis of Conscience* (Atlanta, Commentary Press, 2004), p. 76.

Watchtower publications have an individual's name given as the author. On the other hand, a Catholic knows that from St Peter and the twelve apostles onwards we do know the names of those who have been given the authority to proclaim the Faith to us. This affirms that the Church is not a faceless bureaucracy, but a family, each member of which is known by name by God.

No individuality of thought

Because a Jehovah's Witness is obliged to accept what the Watchtower tells them to believe without question, he will accept no interpretation or understanding of the Scriptures other than that given to them by the Watchtower Society; individual members are not permitted to have their own thoughts about the Scriptures, and can be disfellowshipped[4] if they do:

> Thus the Bible is an organizational book and belongs to the Christian congregation as an organisation, [i.e. the Watchtower], not to individuals, regardless of how sincerely they may believe that they can interpret the Bible.
> *The Watchtower 1/10/1967*, p. 587

Their followers are not allowed to question Watchtower teachings:

> We should eat and digest and assimilate what is set before us, without shying away from parts of the food because it may not

---

[4] Disfellowshippment is a disciplinary procedure that will be discussed in Chapter 23.

> suit the fancy of our mental taste.... We should meekly go along with the Lord's theocratic organization and wait for further clarification, rather than balk at the first mention of a thought unpalatable to us and proceed to quibble and mouth our criticisms and opinions as though they were worth more than the slave's provision of spiritual food. Theocratic ones will appreciate the Lord's visible organisation and not be so foolish as to put against Jehovah's channel their own human reasoning and sentiment and personal feelings.
>
> *The Watchtower 1/2/1952,* pp.79-80

Disagreement with Watchtower teachings is definitely frowned upon, and can also lead to disfellowshipment. Only the Watchtower is allowed to alter the organisation's teachings:

> The Society states that if a doctrine is wrong, then it will in its own time, officially alter the belief. Until then the belief or doctrine must be accepted. To try and hasten this process or expose the false teaching is termed 'running ahead, at worst, apostasy.[5]

By this policy the Watchtower is acknowledging that it gets its beliefs and doctrines wrong, but is expecting its followers to believe and abide by them in the meantime.

---

[5] Trevor Willis, *Can Jehovah's Witnesses Survive?* (Kindle edition), location 818.

To read the Bible without Watchtower interpretation is to invite 'disaster':

> From time to time, there have arisen from among the ranks of Jehovah's people those, who, like the original Satan, have adopted an independent, faultfinding attitude.... They say that it is sufficient to read the Bible exclusively, either alone or in small groups at home. But, strangely, through such 'Bible reading', they have reverted right back to the apostate doctrines that commentaries by Christendom's clergy were teaching 100 years ago.
> *The Watchtower 15/8/1981*

This is an interesting and important passage. The Watchtower is here claiming for itself the authority to teach the Scriptures truthfully and 'infallibly', which the Catholic Church also claims. The question is, who has the right to make the claim? Who has been given the authority to do so? The Watchtower makes this claim for itself. The Church's claim rests on receiving her commission from Christ himself: 'He who hears you hears me' (Luke 10:16) and 'Go into all nations teaching and baptising in the name of the Father, Son and Holy Spirit' (Matthew 28:19, 20). The writings of the Early Church bear witness that all Christians saw the Catholic Church (a name first used by St Ignatius of Antioch, circa 100) as the true authority commissioned by Jesus himself to transmit the Faith to succeeding generations.

The passage also makes the further point that if we do read the Bible without Watchtower interpretation, then we will be drawn to interpret it in the same way that the Church has been teaching, not only for the last 100 years, but for the last 2,000 years. The Witnesses no longer meet in these small groups, perhaps because the Watchtower recognised that they could lead to more independence of thought.

By what authority?

Some Catholics might feel that the Catholic Church, too, is authoritarian in the same way, since it defines what we are to believe. What is the difference, and whose authority can we accept? Reading the *Catechism of the Catholic Church* will give an answer. This Catechism draws on two thousand years of the Church's teaching, of prayerful meditation, of confrontation with opinions which oppose her teaching. The Church recognises that she, and her members, are on a journey, a pilgrimage, of exploration of the Faith once given to the apostles and prophets, and is humbly aware that she has been given the Holy Spirit and assurance that she will never teach anything that is in contradiction to that deposit of faith. The gates of hell will never prevail against her (Matthew 16:18); whoever hears her hears Christ (Luke 10:16). She has been given authority to go and teach by Jesus Christ himself (Matthew 28:18-20).

The Watchtower has been given no such authority. The Watchtower is correct when it says that we need help in interpreting the Bible; there does have to be an authority with the mandate to interpret Scripture, and that authority is given to the Church whose Book, as we have seen, it is. The Watchtower is living proof of how the Scriptures can be distorted by those who set themselves up as the only true interpreters of the Scriptures, outside of the Church.

How did the Watchtower come to consider itself as the only true authority competent to interpret the Scriptures?

Beginnings of the Watchtower Organisation

The organisation came into being in order to study the Bible. Its founder, Charles Taze Russell, when he was 18 years old, organised a Bible Study group in Pittsburgh, Pennsylvania, in the late 1800s. He was heavily influenced by the Seventh Day Adventists and the Millenarist doctrines gaining popularity at that time. From that Bible Study group emerged the Bible Students, which was later renamed the Watchtower Bible and Tract Society. However, because they rejected the Biblical scholarship and teachings of the previous two thousand years, the organisation developed methods of studying the Bible that profoundly distorted the Scriptures and this trend became even more pronounced under his successor as President of the Society, 'Judge'[6] Rutherford.

Selective application

One curious method the Watchtower has is to assert that certain parts of the Scriptures that apply only to certain people. In this way it says that all Scripture is for our instruction, but yet reserves sections of it to a few people only, excluding the vast majority from the divine promises God holds out to us.

---

[6] Joseph Rutherford was admitted to the bar at the age of 22 and began to practise law, but never held an official appointment as Judge; he awarded himself the title after he stood in as a judge on a couple of occasions.

For example, Colossians is written to the Christians at Colossae. It speaks of 'the hope reserved for you in heaven' (Colossians 1:5), but this, according to the Watchtower, is a hope reserved for only a few, the 144,000. However, all Witnesses are expected to follow the exhortations in Chapter 3, without ever receiving the eternal life with God that is their goal.

Selectivity

The Watchtower Society is also very selective as to which texts it uses in support of its doctrines. If texts contradict its teachings, then it uses various methods to overcome the problem. It can render the texts to make them fit its own doctrines; it can so water down the texts to make them almost meaningless; it can even so explain the texts away that they end up, according to the Watchtower's interpretation, saying exactly the opposite of what the text says.

The Watchtower believes that God reveals his truths gradually, but in practice it applies this principle only when it changes its own teachings, which have changed considerably from the time of Charles Taze Russell, but not when it comes to the development of doctrine in the Church. W.C. Stevenson[7] says that the Watchtower believes that every single word of the Bible was written by God, so every single word has equal value. It does not see the development of understanding within the Bible itself.

The Bible is a whole library of books of different genres, from history, poetry, prophecy, etc., but the Watchtower does not distinguish between these different types. It treats the Bible as a flat surface, ignoring the

---

[7] W. C. Stevenson, *The Inside Story of Jehovah's Witnesses*, (New York City, Hart Publishing Company, 1967), p. 39.

development of the People of Israel in their relationship with God over three and a half millennia. We shall see many instances of this when we discuss such doctrines as existence of the soul and life after death, for example.

Many translations

Another curious tactic of the Watchtower is to use a multiplicity of translations of the Scriptures. These can include translations done by serious Scripture scholars, nowadays with Catholic and Protestants collaborating, and also with Catholic editions that include all the books of the Bible, when some were removed at the Reformation. It can also include translations done by individuals with a particular axe to grind, or translations, such as the *New World Translation* (NWT), done by the Watchtower Society itself, that is 'translated' to fit in with its own particular teachings and doctrines.

The New World Translation

The New World Translation was made between 1950 and 1961 by Nathan Knorr, the President), Fred Franz, Albert Schroeder, George Gangas and Milton Henschel. Only Franz knew Greek and Hebrew. The others had no formal training in any biblical language. Franz himself studied classical Greek for two years, but not biblical Greek, and taught himself Hebrew for a year, so his grasp of the Greek of the New Testament and of Hebrew cannot be considered of the truly scholarly level necessary for a genuine translation of the Bible, as a transcript of his trial testimony at the Scottish Court of Sessions, November 1954, attests:

Q. Have you also made yourself familiar with Hebrew?
A. Yes...
Q. So that you have a substantial linguistic apparatus at your command?
A. Yes, for use in my Biblical work.
Q. I think you are able to read and follow the Bible in Hebrew, Greek, Latin, Spanish, Portuguese, German and French?
A. Yes. (*Pursuer's Proof,* p. 7)...
Q. You, yourself, read and speak Hebrew, do you not?
A. I do not speak Hebrew.
Q. You do not?
A. No.
Q. Can you, yourself, translate that into Hebrew?
A. Which?
Q. That fourth verse of the second chapter of Genesis?
A. You mean here?
Q. Yes?
A. No, I wouldn't attempt to do that. (*Pursuer's Proof,* pp. 102, 103)

A qualified teacher of Hebrew stated that this verse was a simple exercise that an average first-or-second-year student would have had no trouble in translating.[8] When I cited this trial transcription to a Witness, The Watchtower had obviously been made aware of it; and he replied that this was only a small part of a long court testimony. Nevertheless, this extract does deal with the relevant question and is supported by further evidence.

---

[8] E. C. Gruss, ed., *We Left Jehovah's Witnesses* (P&R Publishing Co., 1974), pp. 74, 75.

Moreover, *The New World* translation was made to fit Watchtower teachings, not a genuine and accurate translation of the original texts. Given that only one member of the board of 'translators' had even a smattering of Greek and Hebrew, it was possibly done simply by using interlinear Hebrew/English and Greek/English versions.

Of course, new translations will continue to be done, and we can use different translations for different purposes. The *Living Bible*, for example, does not pretend to be an accurate translation, and is almost a transliteration, but by putting things in different ways it is legitimate to use it in prayer and *lectio divina* (prayerful reading of the Scriptures), and it can bring a new freshness to our understanding. On the other hand, when we want a translation that is as accurate as possible, then we can turn to the Revised Standard Version, for example, or the New Jerusalem Bible, or the New American Bible, all of which have very good notes on the text, and many others. It is different when the NWT purports to be an accurate translation and not one that deliberately reflects its own doctrines, and in the process mistranslates many words and passages. No genuine Bible scholar uses the NWT.

Causing confusion

It is difficult to know why the Watchtower muddies the waters in this way, except to confuse and cast doubt. If it can show that a limited number of (dubious) translations agree with the organisation, and puts its version on a par with genuine translations, then it can claim some legitimacy. It can also imply, with such a multiplicity of translations, that Christians are confused as to the truth of the Scriptures and their interpretation of them. It can then put forward its own certainty of the right way of understanding the Scriptures as the only way to understand them. By using a multiplicity of translations it can also subtly bring the listener to the conclusion that orthodox translations are the ones that distort the meaning of the text, and only those that support the Watchtower doctrines are the correct ones.

Since it says it can prove their doctrines from the one that you are using, then don't get drawn into a doubtful one.

Waiting 1900 Years for the truth?

One question you could put to the Jehovah's Witnesses is that, why, when Jesus promised that he would be with his Church to the end of time, he should wait for nearly 1900 years to tell us the 'truth'? Their answer is that they are not following Watchtower teachings, but the Bible, unlike 1900 years of false teaching from the Church, but as I hope to show, this is just not the case.

Other sources

In its books and pamphlets, the Watchtower makes abundant use of other sources to make its points, but its use of these must be treated with great care. With the Internet, it is usually very easy to go to the sources themselves and read the whole text for oneself – often the Watchtower takes passages out of context, which when read in their entirety give a completely different picture to that painted by the organisation.

It is very enlightening, also, to know something about the authors of the works quoted. For example, in their pamphlet *'Should You Believe in the Trinity?'* the Watchtower quotes from Arthur Weigall, who does not believe in the Scriptures as God's Word, and who sees 99% of the New Testament as based on paganism. Not an authority in whom to place too much reliance. He even debunks doctrines in which the Watchtower believes!

The Watchtower discourages Witnesses from reading these books and sources for themselves, but to rely only on their own publications for quotations from other sources; it can even disfellowship them for doing so. Instead, Witnesses are told that only the Watchtower can give their followers 'meat in due season', for it has done the hard work of research for them so that it is unnecessary for them to go to the originals for themselves:

> You may think of study as hard work, as involving heavy research. But in Jehovah's organisation it is not necessary to spend a lot of time and energy in research, for there are brothers in the organisation who are assigned to do that very thing, to help you who do not have so much time for this, these preparing the good material in the *Watchtower* and other publications of the Society.
> *The Watchtower 1/6/1967,* p. 338

This means that Witnesses aren't able to research the sources for themselves, and to make an independent judgment of their reliability. If they did, they would find that more often than not the quotations are taken out of context, and do not bear the meaning put on them by the Watchtower. When I indicated that I had done such research on the sources used in their pamphlet on the Trinity, following a visit from them, the Jehovah's Witness was quite puzzled as to why I needed to do that, and asked me why I had done so. I replied that I had found the use of the Watchtower sources was deceptive and I wanted to find out the full texts for myself. I for my part was bemused that she herself found it incomprehensible that anyone should want or need to do this research. In fact, Witnesses would be disfellowshipped if they read non-Watchtower writings or books that question its teachings.

Studying their source texts

The Watchtower uses a stock of Biblical texts to support its teachings, and these texts will be brought out in any meeting with Witnesses. When explaining its teachings, therefore, I will give these texts and the Watchtower interpretation, and also give a Catholic response to them, to show that there are alternative interpretations to that given by the Watchtower.

CHAPTER 3

USING THE CHURCH FATHERS

In its literature the Watchtower increasingly goes to the Early Church Fathers (those writing in the first 400 years of the Church), to show that they did not teach what the Catholic Church now teaches. In this the organisation is very selective, choosing only those passages that suit its purpose, so if you meet with this practice it is important to go to the writings of the Fathers themselves. With the Internet, and with the many books on the Fathers and the writings of the Fathers being published now, this is easy to do.

The use of the writings of the Early Church Fathers by the Watchtower is a curious one. In *'Let your Kingdom Come'* Chapter 10, it traces what it sees as the falling away of the Church from what it considers the pure primitive faith of the Church after the death of St John at the end of the first century. It asserts that the Early Church immediately began teaching such doctrines as the Trinity and the divinity of Christ, which it alleges were not taught by the apostles. The logical thing, then, would be for it to demonstrate that the Early Fathers reflected these beliefs in their writings. But the Watchtower also trawls such sources as Catholic encyclopaedias and atheistic commentators to prove that the Fathers did *not* teach such doctrines as these! They cannot have it both ways. Either the Early Church did believe these enduring teachings of the Catholic Church or they did not.

Development of Doctrine

Reading the Fathers, it is clear that they did indeed teach what the Catholic Church now teaches, although of course there is a development and an ever deeper understanding by the Church of the deposit of faith given to the Church by Christ. Also, it can be couched in ways unfamiliar to a modern reader, using different terms to those we use nowadays. Cardinal Newman, for example, was drawn into the Catholic Church when, reading the Fathers, he realised that the faith they expressed was found only in the Catholic Church, but that there is also a development of doctrine that is never in contradiction to the Biblical foundation.

This is in contrast to the Watchtower. It has a very limited body of doctrine, but its teachings have changed, rather than developed, over the years, most noticeably with its teaching on the Second Coming of Christ, which will be examined in Chapter 16. When it does change its teachings, this is presented as being 'new light' for its followers.

Taught by the Apostles

Is it true, as the Watchtower claims, that there was an abrupt break between the teaching of the apostles and their disciples? No. The earliest of the Church Fathers sat at the feet of the apostles themselves. For example, St

Ignatius of Antioch was taught by St John, and possibly also by St Peter and St Paul, and he carefully passed on that teaching to those who came after him. St Clement of Rome was a disciple of St Peter and St Mark, and became the third Pope. St Polycarp knew St Ignatius, who encouraged him towards his own martyrdom - and so on. There is an unbroken chain of Catholic teaching from the apostles themselves. As St Irenaeus wrote concerning St Clement of Rome, third in succession to St Peter:

> He had seen the apostles and associated with them, and still had their preaching sounding in his ears and their tradition before their eyes – and not he alone, for there were many still left in his time who had been taught by the apostles.[9]

This passage raises some important points. In the very early days the apostles taught by preaching rather than by written texts. These will have existed in the form of letters (e.g. St Paul's) and in gospels, e.g. St Mark, and the first draft of St Matthew's Gospel, but not many congregations would have had a text – everything had to be written by hand and then circulated gradually through the Christian congregations and read out during the Eucharistic celebrations. At that time, when the Scriptures are mentioned, these would have been the Old Testament.

The passage also speaks of 'tradition'. As we have seen, from the very beginning the Church relied on both Scripture and Tradition – it was never a 'Bible only', a 'Scripture only' Church, which in itself is not a scriptural teaching and nowhere appears in the Bible.

---

[9] St Irenaeus, *Against the Heresies,* 3.3.3.

What is tradition, and what does it mean? Scripture itself attests to tradition:

> So then, brethren, stand firm and hold to the traditions which you were taught by us, either by word of mouth or by letter
> (2 Thessalonians 2:15).

> Be imitators of me, as I am of Christ. I commend you because you remember me in everything and maintain the traditions even as I have delivered them to you
> (1 Corinthians 11:1-2).

The beginning of St Luke's Gospel also gives a hint of this:

> Since many have undertaken to compile a narrative of the events that have been fulfilled among us, just as those who were eyewitnesses from the beginning and ministers of the word have handed them down to us, I too have decided, after investigating everything accurately anew, to write it down in an orderly sequence for you, Most Excellent Theophilus, so that you may realize the certainty of the teachings you have received (1:1-4).

From this we can infer that there must have been accounts of Christ's life being circulated, but the eyewitnesses and ministers of the word would also have given their teaching orally, which Luke now wishes to supplement with a fuller and more orderly account.

St Paul also attests that the apostles carefully handed down and passed on to him the oral tradition of the Eucharist (1 Corinthians 11:23, 24) and the Resurrection appearances (I Corinthians 15:1-6), for example.

CHAPTER 4

IS THE CATHOLIC CHURCH PAGAN?

If the Jehovah's Witness knows you are a Catholic, it will not be long before he accuses the Catholic Church of basing its doctrines on pagan practice and beliefs. Chief among these that the Watchtower alleges, are the pagan origins of the Trinity, the immortality of the soul, the Cross, the celebration of Christmas and birthdays and the halos of saints.

What the ordinary Witness probably does not know, and is not told, is that the founder of the Watchtower, Charles Taze Russell, was fascinated by Egyptology, and at least two of his volumes of his work '*Studies in the Scriptures* ' is devoted to the study of Egyptology, as well as the *'Divine Plan of the Ages'*. However, because Russell's writings are never studied now by the Jehovah's Witnesses, I'm sure that they would dismiss this fact as irrelevant. Nevertheless, he was the founder of the Watchtower organisation, and his influence implicitly lives on; this is important when we consider on what the Watchtower Society is founded.

In *'Thy Kingdom Come'* pp. 342, 362, Russell links the measurements of the pyramid with the date of the purported Second Coming of Christ, something that is of central importance to the Jehovah's Witness belief. The Memorial Stone dedicated to Russell and other faithful followers, installed by the Watchtower Society a few yards from his grave, is in the shape of a pyramid, and bears a 'Cross & Crown' masonic symbol; Russell's remarks are ambiguous as to whether he was himself a Mason. Even as late as 1925 *The Watchtower* was approving of this link with pyramidology:

> In the great Pyramid of Egypt, standing as a silent and inanimate witness of the Lord, is a messenger; and its testimony speaks with great eloquence concerning the divine plan.
> *The Watchtower 15/5/1925,* p. 148[10]

The universality of the Catholic Church

Do we need to be worried about this charge of paganism? Not necessarily. There are two ways to approach the issue. One is that the devil cannot invent anything for himself, and so, when he wishes to start a new religion he corrupts the good to make it a caricature of the best.[11] Of course,

---

[10] Anthony James, *'Knock Knock' Who's There? The Truth about Jehovah's Witnesses,* (www.knockknockbook.co.uk), pp. 100-103, 173-175.

[11] When, as a teenager, I was investigating the Catholic Church, I was at the same time learning about Communism, and was struck by the way many things in communism were similar to practices in the Catholic Church, e.g. communist show trials versus confession, adulation of a supreme leader versus worship of Jesus Christ, a social programme which subordinated the

that false religion will bear some likenesses of the good, which is why many will be seduced by it. Another way to look at it is that the Catholic Church is, as its name states, universal, and all peoples have a place within it. She reaches out to everyone, of whatever nation or culture. She recognises that God has implanted knowledge of himself and of his truth within the heart of every human being, giving them the ability to know and love him (cf. Romans 1:19-20). God prepared the peoples for the coming of Christ not only through his Chosen People, the Jews, so that Jesus could say the Old Testament spoke of him; (John 5:39), but also in the groping of pagan beliefs towards the truth. However, as St Paul goes on to say, that clarity has been obscured and distorted. The Church then has to discern what is true and what is false in other religions. She accepts those elements that speak the truth and which find their fulfilment in Christ, while rejecting whatever is false.

That is why the Church can affirm the true and the good that can be found in other religions or in sincere non-believers who yet seek the good, the true and the beautiful – (cf. CCC 836- 845).

Pagans being prepared for Christ

In fact, it is thrilling to see traces of truth in the religions, myths and beliefs that preceded the coming of Christ. This prepared non-Jewish Gentiles to accept the fullness of truth revealed in Jesus Christ because it would not have been totally alien to them. St Paul recognised this when he addressed the Athenians in the Areopagus; he discerned

---

individual to the state versus the gospel which declared the sacredness of the individual as a child of God. I reasoned that the devil would only ape the best, which was another factor that brought me into the Catholic Church!

the truth that resided within their beliefs, and showed how Jesus was the fulfilment of their searching (see Acts 17:22-33). When a Jehovah's Witness accuses our Church of paganism you might like to point out some facts about Paul's address to the Athenians. When he quotes a poet 'For we too are his offspring' he is quoting Aratus of Soli, a third century B.C. poet from Cilicia, from a poem addressed to Zeus, the chief god of the Greeks. As Paul says, 'What therefore you unknowingly worship, I proclaim to you.'

Again, in his letter to Titus (1:12) St Paul quotes from a Cretan writer, and also calls him a prophet. Paul was well read and recognised that God's inspiration was not limited to Christians and Jews. We do not have to be defensive about the fact that God has revealed himself in partial and fragmentary fashion outside the Judeo-Christian tradition; people have sought him with whatever light they have, and St Paul wasn't at all apologetic about it!

Paganism and the Early Church

The young Church was surrounded by paganism, and therefore had to deal with it. This was the world they had to convert to Christ. Some of the great writers of the Early Church were philosophers, and therefore used their training in pagan philosophy to understand the Christian faith, and to explain it to others. Later on, St Thomas Aquinas would use Aristotelian philosophy to great effect in exploring and explaining the Christian faith, while St Augustine was drawn to Plato. He, and the Medieval Church, recognised that God reveals himself to all people of good will, and can speak to every heart that is open to him. In every age, the Church must speak to the people of that time in the language of the times, without in any way compromising the unchanging message of the Gospel.

Restore all things in Christ

This is the Church's mission – to restore, to unite, all things in Christ (cf. Eph 1:10). Therefore from the very beginning, the Church has seen that all things must be sanctified, brought back to God through Christ. St Peter learnt this important lesson. Acts 10 recounts how he received a visit from a devout Roman centurion called Cornelius, who was told by God to go to Peter. Peter himself also received a vision in which he saw a sheet coming down from heaven containing animals that Jews were forbidden to eat. When Peter balked at eating them, he heard the words 'What God has made clean, you are not to call profane.' This helped Peter to accept Cornelius into the Church. It made such an impression on him because he also understood its wider implications, that 'God shows no partiality. Rather, in every nation whoever fears him and acts uprightly is acceptable to him' (Acts 10:34-35).

So later on, Christians were not concerned that Christian festivals sometimes fell on pagan feast days, and that they would sometimes take over temples that had previously been dedicated to pagan gods, to dedicate them now to the worship of the True God.

The early Christians were well able to distinguish between worship of the One True God and the worship of idols, even when there seemed to be similarities between them. St Justin Martyr, for example, in his *First Apology*, goes into even greater detail about these similarities than the Jehovah's Witnesses. He sees them as the imitation by demons of the real truth lived out by Jesus. (See Appendix 1 for an extended reading from Justin Martyr's *Apology*). C.S. Lewis famously said that in Jesus, myth became reality.

Although, during his earthly ministry, the message was first to the Jewish people, Jesus in fact embraced pagans who came to him. He healed the Syrophoenician woman's daughter (Mark 7:24ff), a Samaritan was the hero of his famous parable (Luke10:29ff), he praised the faith of the Roman Centurian (Matt:8:10), and it was a Roman soldier who recognized him as 'the Son of God' at the crucifixion. (Matt 27:54)

So there are two ways of approaching paganism – the attempt to use the best of pagan thought, which does sometimes foreshadow the truth of Jesus Christ, while rejecting the pagan myths of gods, which, while bearing similarities to the Christian faith, also bear gross distortions and perversions which must be, and were, rejected by the Christian Church. It must be admitted, though, that in some countries pagan practices do still persist in parallel with the Catholic faith, and people do need better teaching of their faith to bring them to trust in Jesus alone.

The Magi

There is a story in the Gospels that plots this progression from paganism to Christ. St Matthew relates the journey of the Magi, the Wise Men, from their pagan homeland to the feet of Jesus. 'The heavens declare the glory of God', they were made by his hands, but pagan religions had made them their god, and sought to find truths in the heavens by which to guide their lives. It was a deficient understanding, but God seeks and finds us where we are to guide us to where he is. The Wise Men started off their journey by the omens they read in the heavens, but they could go only so far by their light. At one point they had to seek a closer light, within the pages of the Old Testament. The Old Covenant brought them to the feet of Christ, to worship him and lay their riches before him. Pagan faith and God's revelation of himself in the Old Testament had brought them to the fullness of revelation of God himself in the person of Jesus Christ. They could no longer return by the way they had come. That journey had fulfilled its purpose. They now had to return to their homeland by a new, different way, the Way of the Gospel.

Paganism in Watchtower teaching

What the Watchtower totally rejects is that its religion has any relationship with pagan thought, which, as I have shown, is untrue. A case could be made that its religion still has pagan elements in it, which shows that a case can be made for anything!

For example, the word 'Paradise' is of Persian and therefore of pagan origin, although adopted into the New Testament.

While insisting that they worship only Jehovah, Jehovah's Witnesses believe that Jesus is 'a god', (see John 1:1, NWT) not sharing the same nature as Jehovah God; that angels are gods, as are men. Although they vehemently reject the idea, this surely is polytheism, even though they insist they worship only Jehovah God.

The *stauros*, or stake, on which they assert Jesus was crucified, bears more of a resemblance to pagan totems than the cross they reject.

I would like to close this section by recommending strongly that, as well as having a well-translated Bible with good footnotes and study guides, that you also have a copy of the *Catechism of the Catholic Church*. These two books will be the richest possible store from which to deepen your understanding of your Catholic Faith, and are indispensable tools that will expose the errors of the Watchtower. Further, the *Catechism of the Catholic Church* is so imbued with the Scriptures that it could be seen as a commentary on the Scriptures.

PART 2

CATHOLIC DOCTRINES UNDER FIRE

You might have already told the Jehovah's Witness that you are a Christian, and they might gather, from your front room, perhaps with a Crucifix or a statue visible, that you are Catholic. They will probably start attacking/discussing the central beliefs of our Christian Faith – the Trinity, the Divinity of Jesus Christ, his Crucifixion, the Holy Spirit. These are the doctrines that we will discuss next.

CHAPTER 5

THE TRIUNE GOD, FATHER, SON AND HOLY SPIRIT

The Trinity is at the very heart of Christian faith, and it is a truth that comes under great attack by the Watchtower. According to them, the doctrine of the Trinity is of pagan origin, and they trawl through a series of pagan religions in search of trios of gods. Of course, the One God, Father, Son and Holy Spirit, is not three gods, but one, so this search is totally irrelevant.

The Most Holy Trinity, Father, Son and Holy Spirit, are three Persons in One God. This reality, revealed implicitly by Jesus Christ and proclaimed by the Catholic Church, is vehemently rejected by the Watchtower. It has produced a pamphlet entitled '*Should You Believe in the Trinity?*' The answer of every Christian should be a resounding 'Yes'! As the Watchtower agrees, it has been and is the central doctrine of the Church from the very beginning and for most denominations. It is therefore vital, as the Watchtower acknowledges, that we should know the truth of the nature of God, as he has revealed himself to us.

'Should you believe in the Trinity?'

If a Jehovah's Witness gives this pamphlet to a Catholic, he or she may be very disturbed, because the pamphlet quotes from Catholic priests, theologians and encyclopaedias. It gives the impression that reputable sources such as the New Catholic Encyclopaedia actually contradicts the teachings of the Church. However, this is not so. The Watchtower doctors the quotations very carefully – you may notice the use of dots where sections have been omitted; when the full passage or sentence is restored, the meaning is very different. I will give examples of this as I discuss what the pamphlet says. Some of the points it makes are:

- The mystery of the Trinity is an incomprehensible confusion.
- Many theologians, including Catholic sources, disagree with it.
- The doctrine is not found in the Early Church Fathers
- Rather, it was 'made up' in the 4th century
- It was adopted from paganism.

The mystery of the Trinity is an incomprehensible confusion

To the Watchtower the truth of the Trinity is a confusion, and they quote Pope John Paul 11 speaking of 'the inscrutable mystery of God the Trinity.' The Trinity, it says, is beyond the grasp of human reason, and it describes the difficulty priests have in explaining it. However, to allege that seminarians go to their professors and ask 'But how does one preach the Trinity?' is not an indication of confusion, as the Watchtower interprets it, but of the majesty and awesomeness of the subject.

To justify its position, the Watchtower misunderstands the word 'mystery' and gives it the purely secular meaning of something that is incomprehensible and unknowable. What it does not say is that the word 'mystery' is itself a Scriptural word, which has been used by both the Catholic and Orthodox Churches ever since New Testament times. The NWT renders the word as 'sacred secret'. The Catechism defines mysteries as 'hidden in God, which can never be known unless they are revealed by God' (CCC 237).

The Church readily acknowledges that she can never fully comprehend the mysteries of God. If the Scriptures say 'Who can understand the mind of the Lord?' then surely we will have greater difficulty in understanding the being of God Himself. Jesus himself said that 'No-one knows the Son except the Father, and no-one knows the Father except the Son, and those to whom the Son chooses to reveal him' (Luke 10:22). God is beyond our finite human reason, but not in opposition to it. He would not be God if he was fully comprehensible to the limited faculties of our human mind; on the contrary, he is far beyond all that we can comprehend by human means, but we do not have to rely on human means. He has poured the Holy Spirit into our hearts so that what cannot be fully grasped by our minds can be apprehended by our faith.

In fact, the Watchtower acknowledges that God exceeds our reason. In *Reasoning From the Scriptures,* p. 148, it states 'Our minds cannot fully comprehend [the eternity of God. But that is not a sound reason for rejecting it.' And speaking of God as Creator: 'Should we really expect to understand everything about a Person who is so great that he could bring into existence the universe, with all its intricate design and stupendous size?' (*ibid.*, p.149). Why can it not accept the incomprehensible, unfathomable nature and being of God as Father, Son and Holy Spirit, is beyond our natural human reason, also?

'Many theologians, including Catholic sources, disagree with it.'

It is important to know something of the sources the Watchtower uses. For example, *The Paganism in Our Christianity* is by Arthur Weigall, who, as we have seen, besides rejecting the Trinity, also rejects as pagan 28 further Christian beliefs, such as the 12 apostles (derived from the Zodiac), the name of Mary as the Mother of Jesus (it bears vague resemblance to the names of pagan goddesses), Jesus's temptation in the wilderness (Pan tempting Jupiter), right through the life death and resurrection of Jesus. So what credence can we give him when the Watchtower cites him as an authority on Christian belief?

Likewise, the Yale professor, Washburn Hopkins, whom it quotes also sees the whole of Christianity as derived from paganism. He sees baptism, fasting, the hope of immortality and resurrection, for example, as pre-Christian and derived also from Buddhism (*Origin and Evolution of Religion*, Chapter 20*)*, so again, it is unsurprising that he gives the Trinity a pagan origin.

Of more concern to Catholics is the allegation that Catholic sources and theologians are quoted to portray the doctrine of the Trinity as being mired in confusion, and that many Catholics disagree with it. But all is not as it seems. For example, on page 4 it quotes from *The Catholic Encyclopaedia,* 'A dogma so mysterious presupposes a divine revelation', which of course is perfectly true, and it is Jesus Christ Himself who has revealed it to us. The full quotation, continues:

> When the fact of revelation, understood in its full sense as the speech of God to man, is no longer admitted, the rejection of the doctrine follows as a necessary consequence.

Hans Kung is also quoted, but the Holy See has withdrawn his faculties to teach as a Catholic theologian.

God transcends human thinking

The booklet quotes many instances of priests and seminarians saying how difficult it is to preach on the Trinity, and I am sure that is true! But again, this does not negate the reality of God's being, but rather highlights how difficult it is for us to put into human speech something that is so far beyond our human understanding. However, what Jesus invites us to do is to live within the mystery of God's being, to understand in a way that we may not be able to express adequately, but that we do indeed live within the family life of God Himself, Who is Love, love given and received and poured out in our hearts; then we will 'have the strength to comprehend with all the holy ones what is the breadth and length and height and depth, and to know the love of Christ *that surpasses knowledge*, so that you may be filled with all the fullness of God' (Ephesians 3:18,19), (italics added). Our destiny is to share in the very life of God in heaven, and that process begins, here and now, on earth.

It is not taught by the Early Church Fathers

Wrong! Robert Finnerty, author of *Jehovah's Witnesses on Trial'* describes (pp. 151,152), how he wrote to the Watchtower 'requesting specific references for each of the Church Fathers cited in their pamphlet. 'In response,' he wrote, 'I received a letter and photocopies of selected pages from a single book, Alvin Lamson's *The Church of the First Three Centuries'* [which he reproduces]. 'No other materials or direct references to the works of the Fathers themselves were enclosed.' Alvin Lamson was a Unitarian, so therefore did not believe in the Trinity any more than the Watchtower. Moreover, Finnerty found that the so-called quotes from the Fathers were, rather, Lamson's interpretation of them. The Watchtower authorities had presumably not read the sources themselves.

Every one of the Fathers mentioned in the pamphlet believed in the Trinity.

Rather, it was 'made up' in the 4th century

This stands history on its head. The Council of Nicaea opened on 20 May 325 A.D., attended by 312 bishops from Egypt, Palestine, Syria, Asia Minor, Africa, Spain, Gaul and Italy, so not the 'fraction of the total' alleged by the Watchtower. To quote P.C. Thomas[12]:

> It was a spectacle for the eyes of any beholder. Remember that just ten years before, Christians were on the run under constant persecution. Some of those bishops who had gathered there, bore scars

---

[12] P.C. Thomas, *General Councils of the Church* (USA St Pauls Publications, 1993), p. 10.

of torture. There were bishops who were lame or half blind. Many of them were living saints, whose very shadow had cured illness. No wonder that the people of Nicaea feasted their eyes on this unearthly spectacle of the Council Fathers.

They had assembled there to come to some decision on the doctrines taught by a bishop, Arius, who taught the following:

- The Son of God is not of one substance with the Father
- The Son of God is not equal to the Father
- The Son of God is not co-eternal with the Father
- The Son of God is created and therefore is not God

In the words of P.C. Thomas:

> When Arius began to preach these unheard-of doctrines from the pulpit of his church, a few people complained to Alexander, bishop of Alexandria. The bishops' first act was to call a meeting of some bishops and priests to hear from the very lips of Arius his new teachings. In this first public disputation, Arius was routed. He received a reprimand and was told that he should not preach any longer in the church[13].

---

[13] P.C. Thomas, *General Councils of the Church*, p. 12.

So in the fourth century it was not the doctrine of the Trinity that was new, but the very teachings of the Jehovah's Witnesses who could be called neo-Arians.

It was adopted from paganism.

If the Watchtower authorities had read the writings of St Justin Martyr for themselves, they would have found a wealth of material that they could have used, selectively, to support their case. In his *First Apology*, Justin details the similarities between the Greek gods and the life of Jesus:

> And when we say also that the Word, who is the first-birth of God, was produced without sexual union, and that He, Jesus Christ, our Teacher, was crucified and died, and rose again, and ascended into heaven, we propound nothing different from what you believe regarding those whom you esteem sons of Jupiter.... And what of the emperors who die among yourselves, whom you deem worthy of deification, and in whose behalf you produce some one who swears he has seen the burning Caesar rise to heaven from the funeral pyre?.... Moreover, the Son of God called Jesus, even if only a man by ordinary generation, yet, on account of His wisdom, is worthy to be called the Son of God; for all writers call God the Father of men and gods. And if we assert that the Word of God was born of God in a peculiar manner, different from ordinary generation, let this, as said above, be no extraordinary thing to you, who say that

> Mercury is the angelic word of God. But if any one objects that He was crucified, in this also He is on a par with those reputed sons of Jupiter of yours, who suffered as we have now enumerated. [14]

It is important to understand Justin's argument. He is making comparisons with the pagan gods to make the point that the Christian faith is not totally alien to pagan beliefs, but he is definitely not saying that the events of Christ's life, death and resurrection were derived from pagan sources. Elsewhere in his *Apology*, he shows how all the events of Christ's life were foretold in the Old Testament, and then said that the demons, seeing that, made up their myths to mislead people. That the Gentiles were also being prepared for the coming of Jesus Christ through their myths, meant that when the Good News was preached to them they had no difficulty in accepting Jesus as their Lord and Saviour, true God and true man, even if they had not read the Hebrew Scriptures.

The truth about the Trinity

Catholics actually agree with much of what the Watchtower alleges! We agree that the Trinity is a mystery – in the Scriptural sense, but not in the Watchtower sense. We agree with Pope John Paul 11 that it is 'the inscrutable mystery' and that it is 'beyond the grasp of human reason', which is why we affirm that it was revealed to us by Jesus himself. In fact, is the Watchtower not defeating its own argument by saying that the Church made it up when it is also agreeing that it is beyond the grasp of human reason! In other words, no human being could make up the doctrine

---

[14] See Appendix 1 for an extended text of this passage.

of the Trinity. Here is the extended text taken from *The Catholic Encyclopaedia,* which is quoted selectively in the pamphlet:

> Although there are intimations of it in the Old Testament, the Church has always seen it as being revealed with the coming of Jesus. This he did gradually. First He taught them to recognize in Himself the eternal Son of God. When His ministry was drawing to a close, He promised that the Father would send another Divine Person, the Holy Spirit, in His place. Finally after His resurrection, He revealed the doctrine in explicit terms, bidding them "go and teach all nations, baptizing them in the name of the Father, and of the Son, and of the Holy Ghost" (Matthew 28:18). The force of this passage is decisive. That "the Father" and "the Son" are distinct Persons follows from the terms themselves, which are mutually exclusive. The mention of the Holy Spirit in the same series, the names being connected one with the other by the conjunctions "and... and" is evidence that we have here a Third Person co-ordinate with the Father and the Son; it excludes altogether the supposition that the Apostles understood the Holy Spirit not as a distinct Person, but as God viewed in His action on creatures.
>
> The phrase "in the name" (*eis to onoma*) affirms alike the Godhead of the Persons and their unity of nature. Among the Jews

and in the Apostolic Church the Divine name was representative of God. He who had a right to use it was invested with vast authority: for he wielded the supernatural powers of Him whose name he employed. It is incredible that the phrase "in the name" should be employed here, were not all the Persons mentioned equally Divine. Moreover, the use of the singular, "name," and not the plural, shows that these Three Persons are that One omnipotent God in whom the Apostles believed. Indeed the unity of God is so fundamental a tenet alike of the Hebrew and of the Christian religion, and is affirmed in such countless passages of the Old and New Testaments, that any explanation inconsistent with this doctrine would be altogether inadmissible.

God prepares us for his revelations

God doesn't suddenly spring surprises on us, unprepared. In the Old Testament he is gradually revealing himself. There are intimations of the Triune nature of God from the very first pages of the Bible:

> In the beginning God created the heavens and the earth. Now the earth was a formless void, there was darkness over the deep, and God's spirit hovered over the water. God said, 'Let there be light, and there was light' (Genesis 1:1-3).

Here we see God the Creator, his Word spoken and his Spirit who gives life. It is the Trinity in action. When

God comes to create man he uses a different form of words from the rest of his creating work: 'Let us make man in our image'. Many commentaries say that this plural refers to the divine beings who compose God's heavenly court. Maybe so, but we are made in God's image, not his heavenly court and the use of the plural here could also be an intimation of the Trinity. Two names of God, Adonai and Elohim, are both in the plural.

The Church has long seen in the visit of the three strangers to Abraham (Genesis 18) an intimation of the Trinity, especially as Abraham addresses them as 'My lord' in the singular.(Gn 18:3) and in the threefold 'Holy, Holy Holy' in Isaiah's vision of God in the Temple. (Isaiah 6:3)

It was in 538 B.C. when the Jews returned from exile in Babylon and rebuilt the Temple (2nd Temple period) to the birth of Christ that Jewish sages began meditating on the mysterious vision of Daniel 7:13-14 of 'one like a Son of Man' 'who is mysteriously more than human' (Jerusalem Bible note k) The books of Esdras and Enoch (which are included in the Orthodox Bible) explored this vision in great depth and Jesus himself applied this title to himself. Sadly, the majority of the Temple hierarchy were unable to recognise the Son of Man in a jobbing carpenter from Nazareth.

This has answered a question of mine; how was it, if the Jews had such a strong monotheistic faith in the oneness of God, that those first Jewish converts were so easily able to accept the divinity of Christ, so compellingly stated in, especially, the letters of St Paul?' This answered my question. In the great Jewish affirmation of faith, the *Shema Israel*, Hear O Israel, the Lord your God is one Lord...' it is not a statement about the inner nature of God but should rather be translated as 'the Lord your God, the only God'. God gradually taught the Jews that he was not just one god among the many gods of the pagans around them. They gradually came to see that there is only one God, the Creator of heaven and earth.

In the Early Church

In the first years of the Church the early believers did not define the Trinity, they lived it, as Catholics have done so ever since. They were baptised 'in the name of the Father, the Son and the Holy Spirit'. They were adamant that they worshipped and adored the One True God, who is Father, Son and Holy Spirit. For example:

> True God. Hence are we called atheists. And we confess that we are atheists, so far as gods of this sort are concerned, but not with respect to the most true God, the Father of righteousness and temperance and the other virtues, who is free from all impurity. But both Him, and the Son (who came forth from Him and taught us these things, and the host of the other good angels who follow and are made like to Him), and the prophetic Spirit, we worship and adore, knowing them in reason and truth, and declaring without grudging to every one who wishes to learn, as we have been taught (Justin Martyr: *Apology*).

Of pagan origin?

The Watchtower's main objection is that the doctrine of the Trinity is pagan in origin, and it goes to great lengths to trawl pre-Christian religions searching for anything that has three 'somethings' in them. However, it quotes no writings that I know of that show that the Church 'proves' the Trinity by referring to pagan sources.

The assertion is made that the doctrine of the Trinity was introduced only in the fourth century. This is incorrect. The first time the term 'Trinity' is used appears in 180 A.D. by St Theophilus of Antioch: 'The three days which were before the luminaries, are types of the Trinity, of God, and His Word, and His wisdom' (*To Autolycus*). The fact that Theophilus uses the term in such a matter-of-fact way, without any qualification or sense that he is coining a new word, surely means that Autolycus would have been familiar with it and that therefore the term was already in current use. Tertullian also uses it about 200 A.D. and in the mid-3rd Century Novation wrote a treatise '*On the Trinity*'; so very early on Christians were firming up their understanding of God as revealed by Jesus Christ by using this term.

The word 'Trinity' not in the Bible

It is true that the word 'Trinity' does not appear in the Scriptures. Neither does the word 'theocracy' and 'classes' for example, or the term 'paradise earth', 'spirit creature' and other terms so beloved of the Jehovah's Witnesses. But the Church would say that the reality of those concepts **is** in the Scriptures. That is what we say of the Trinity. We agree, too, that the Church's understanding of the relationship between the Father, Son and Holy Spirit developed over a period of many years; just as Jesus promised that she would be led into all truth (John 16:13). Even after twenty centuries, the Holy Spirit is still leading us more deeply into the truth, always revealing new depths, new understandings, of the faith delivered once for all to the saints (Jude 2). The Church, in her members, first of all lives out her faith. It is when that lived faith is challenged by unbelievers that the Church must delve more deeply into *what* she believes, and *why* she believes it; then she formulates it to clarify her faith and also to say what is not consistent with that faith.

Taught by Early Christians?

This section in the pamphlet begins with a quotation from *The New International Dictionary of New Testament Theology*: 'Primitive Christianity did not have an explicit doctrine of the Trinity such as was subsequently elaborated in the creeds.' The important word here is 'explicit', because from the very beginning, and starting with the New Testament, the doctrine was there implicitly. It did indeed develop over four centuries for it to take the form it did by 381 A.D.

There are three incidents in the New Testament where the Trinity is manifested: at the Annunciation (Luke 1:26-38) where the will of the Father is made known through the words of the angel, Mary is overshadowed by the Holy Spirit and the Word became flesh; at the Baptism of Christ in the river Jordan (Matthew 3:16-17) when the voice of the Father was heard and the Spirit descended upon Jesus; and at the Transfiguration (Mark 9:2-8) where the voice of the Father is heard, the cloud of the Holy Spirit enveloped them and the divinity of Jesus was revealed.

Just as the New Testament mentioned or showed the Three Persons in several places, so the early Christians invoked Them. Just a few examples of the many that could be cited:

> Do we not have one God and one Christ, and one Spirit of Grace poured out upon us? (St Clement of Rome, circa A.D. 70, *Letter to the Corinthians,* Chapter 46).

> For, as God lives and the Lord Jesus Christ lives and the Holy Spirit, the faith and hope of the elect... (*ibid.*, Chapter 58).

> For this and for all benefits I praise You, I bless You, I glorify You, through the eternal and heavenly High Priest, Jesus Christ, Your beloved Son, through whom be to you with Him and the Holy Spirit glory, now and for all ages to come. Amen.
> (*The Martyrdom of St Polycarp* 14:3)

The Christians of the first three centuries believed in and worshipped the One God, Father, Son and Holy Spirit, but it was only when this belief was challenged and opposed by Arius in the fourth century, that the Church met in a General Council and defined what she believed.

Can Jesus be worshipped?

The Watchtower acknowledges that only God can be worshipped, and therefore the fact that these early Christians are worshipping Jesus and the Holy Spirit equally with the Father shows that they believed in the divinity of Jesus and the Holy Spirit. Since the Watchtower denies the divinity of Jesus it must deny that Jesus is being worshipped equally with the Father. It rightly points out that the Greek '*proskyneo*' means both to worship and to 'bow down before' a person, and therefore whenever the Scriptures describes an obeisance being shown to Jesus it consistently translates '*proskyneo*' as bowing down before or doing obeisance to him, rather than him being worshipped. A Jehovah's Witness said to me that in those cases where Jesus is being worshipped, then he is passing on that worship to his Father – although, of course, that is not what the Scriptures say.

In Revelation 21:8, John said that he 'knelt at the feet of the angel' who was showing him the visions 'to worship him, but he said, 'Don't do that: I am a servant just like you...' Jesus never said that to those who were kneeling at his feet, doing him obeisance, worshipping him during his earthly life. They may not have understood the full import of his divinity, but they were seeing in him someone who was representing God in a unique way. Jesus himself accepted their homage.

Catholic belief

What is the basis of the Christian belief in the Trinity, three Persons in One God? As we have seen, it is a belief that we inherit from the very first days of the Christian Church and from the Scriptures. It is what Jesus tells us of himself, as we shall see. But it is perhaps St John's proclamation that 'God is Love' that holds the secret. Love has to be given and received. God did not become Love after he had created the world, which then gave him something on which to pour out his love. No, his very being is love, and therefore his being is love given and received and poured out for all eternity. The Father pours out his love on his Son, the Son pours out his love on the Father, and that love is Person, the Holy Spirit. The Trinity is relationship, a relationship of Love, and he has invited every single human being he has ever created and will create, to share in that life of love. It is for this that he has created us and this relationship begins here and now, on earth. That is the basis of the Christian message.

CHAPTER 6

JEHOVAH GOD

In 1931, Rutherford renamed the Bible Students 'Jehovah's Witnesses' taking his inspiration from Isaiah 43:10-12. It has remained a distinctive feature of the Jehovah's Witnesses to use this name for God. The name Jehovah is derived from the Hebrew Tetragrammaton יהוה (YHWH). It was first coined by a Benedictine monk in the 6th century, and became popular in early English translations of the Bible. Since the pointing – the consonants - are missing in the tetragrammaton he inserted the consonants of another word for God, *Adonai*, which is the name that the Jews substitute for YHWH when reading from the sacred text. However, the result is an impossible construct in Hebrew.

In the booklet entitled '*The Divine Name That Will Endure Forever*', the Watchtower goes into great detail about the history and the use of the Name. It gives two explanations as to why the Jews do not pronounce the Name, that 'First, a superstitious idea arose among the Jews that it was wrong to say the divine name out loud'; then, 'as time went by, the ancient Hebrew language itself ceased to be spoken in everyday conversation, and in this way the original Hebrew pronunciation of God's name was eventually forgotten' (p. 8). In *Knowledge that Leads to Everlasting Life* p. 24 the Watchtower repeats the charge that 'the Jews superstitiously ceased to pronounce the divine name'. The opposite is the case. It was so sacred to the Jews that eventually only the High Priest was allowed to utter it in the Holy of Holies once a year on the Day of Atonement, which is why no-one now knows exactly how it was pronounced. When reading the Hebrew text and in conversation a Jew will say instead 'Adonai' or HaShem', (the Name), or write G-d, not from superstition but because of the profound reverence they have for the name of God.

The importance of the Name

There are various interpretations of the meaning of the Name; it could be I AM WHO AM, I AM, or HE CAUSES TO BECOME. God is the source, the cause of all that is, and in Himself IS. He alone is pure Being.

The Watchtower rightly points out that to get know a person we need to know his name. In Hebrew understanding, the name denotes a person, his very being, which is why in several places in the Scriptures God will change a person's name, for example, Abram, (the father is exalted), to Abraham, (father of a multitude), and, of course, Simon to Peter, (Rock), to denote a profound change in that person's mission and being. God will also say what a person's name will be, for example, John (God has graced) the Baptist, and above all the name of Jesus – God Saves.

However, in the NWT, the Watchtower goes beyond using the name Jehovah legitimately, when it quotes from the Old Testament, but by also inserting it into the New Testament, where it never was. It gives as its reason for this that St Jerome said that St Matthew 'first of all composed a Gospel of Christ in Judaea in the Hebrew language and characters for the benefit of those of the circumcision who had believed' (*De viris inlustribus,* Chapter 111*).* The Watchtower then says that '[T]his Gospel includes 11 direct quotations of the portions of the Hebrew Scriptures where the Tetragrammaton is found.' No texts have ever been found, of the many hundreds of fragments and copies of the Gospels that are in existence from the very first years of the Christian faith, to support its assertion. It is true that in a Hebrew translation of the New Testament the tetragrammaton is used when quoting from the Old Testament, but the same rule applies. Wherever the tetragrammaton is used or displayed it is pronounced as *Adonai.* In the booklet, the Watchtower reproduces many photos showing the tetragrammaton carved into the walls of synagogues and churches, for example, but there is no problem with the written form; the Watchtower just does not understand that it is never pronounced in the Hebrew.

It asks if Jesus pronounced the Name and suggests that when he read from the scroll of Isaiah in the synagogue at the start of his public ministry, (Luke 4:16-20), he would not have followed 'such an unscriptural tradition' as substituting *Adonai* for YHWH. He most surely did follow the tradition, because when he did indeed pronounce the Name, I AM, and furthermore used it for himself, the Jews picked up stones to stone him (John 8:58, 59). They did not do so in the synagogue. The only time the New Testament records Jesus as using the Name, I AM, is when he uses it for himself, and the Jews, by their reaction, knew what he was doing.

The Watchtower quotes passages where Jesus speaks of the name of God:

> he taught his followers to pray to God: "Let your name be sanctified." (Matthew 6:9) And in prayer on the night before

> his execution he said to his Father: "I have made your name manifest to the men you gave me out of the world...Holy Father, watch over them on account of your own name which you have given me." (John 17:6, 11) (NWT).

What is striking is that in all these examples it is not the name YHWH that Jesus is recorded as uttering but the name of Father, which the Watchtower completely fails to notice. If Jesus thought it was so important for his followers to use the tetragrammaton, then surely he would have told us to use it in the very prayer he gave us, and would have been recorded as using it in his own prayer at the Last Supper. It is also striking that in this quotation, Jesus says that the Father has given His Name, His Nature, to Jesus, another proof of Jesus' divinity.

However, it is the name of *Father* that he has given us to use above all others because this is the name that the first Christians, and Christians ever since, have recognised as being the name above all names that Jesus himself uses. 'God has sent the Spirit of his Son into our hearts: the Spirit that cries, 'Abba, Father' (Galatians 4:6). It is Jesus' own Spirit, the Holy Spirit of Father and Son, within us that utters this name.

We have also been given the name of Jesus, the name above all other names, to proclaim Jesus Christ as Lord, to the glory of the Father (Phil. 2:9-11).

Why does The Watchtower persist in using the name Jehovah God? Undoubtedly, it is for reverence for God, but it also has the implicit result of denying the divinity of Christ. It emphasises the assumed monotheism of God revealed in the Old Testament as opposed to the polytheism of the surrounding nations, but it refuses to accept the development in our understanding of the nature of God revealed by Christ Jesus. In the New Testament it is at the Name of Jesus that every knee shall bow. By revealing the New Name, Abba, Father, Jesus shows that he is introducing us into a wholly new relationship with God; we have become part of the family of God, and as we have seen, God himself is a family relationship. Thus there is the tendency, that by using the name Jehovah, it makes God more distant than the names of Father and Jesus and Holy Spirit, the Name of the only God.

CHAPTER 7

JESUS CHRIST, SON OF GOD

Recently, a Jehovah's Witness came round with a leaflet which asked what one thought of the Bible. What immediately struck me was that there was mention at all of Jesus in the leaflet. For a Catholic, the whole of the Bible is about Jesus Christ; Jesus himself said that the Scriptures bore testimony to him (John 5:39), and on the road to Emmaus he went through the Scriptures of the Old Testament, showing how they bore witness to him (Luke 24:27).

In the Old Testament we see the Israelite nation being prepared for the coming of the Messiah; there are prophesies about his coming; there are 'antitypes' of the Messiah – Jeremiah foreshadows the Man of Sorrows, for example, and Moses the Lawgiver foreshadows Jesus, the Lawgiver of the New Law of love. The New Testament proclaims his coming, the fulfilment of the Old Testament. In the words of St Augustine, the Old Testament foreshadows the New Testament, and the Old Testament is fulfilled in the New. In producing a leaflet on the Bible with no mention of Jesus is an indication of the lesser place the Watchtower gives to him in their beliefs. He is their field marshall under Jehovah of Armies (*Worldwide Peace and Security under the Prince of Peace 1986*), and it specifically rejects the place of Jesus as the sole mediator between God and men:

> Likewise, the Greater Moses, Jesus Christ, is not the Mediator between Jehovah God and all mankind. He is the mediator ... to only 144,000 members.
> *Worldwide Security Under the Prince of Peace,* p. 10[15]

Instead, the Watchtower, the 'faithful and discreet slave', is now the mediator between God and its faithful followers: 'Come to Jehovah's organisation for salvation' (*The Watchtower*, 15/11/1981). The Scriptures say 'For of all the names in the world given to men, this is the only one [Jesus] by which we can be saved' (Acts 4:12), something that the Watchtower rejects.

Catholics have sometimes been accused of putting mediators between Jesus and ourselves: we call Mary Mediatrix; our priests administer the sacraments to us, so what is the difference between the Church's teaching and that of the Watchtower?

The difference is that the Watchtower has taken away Christ's mediation and reserved it only for the 144,000. In the Church we share in Christ's mediation. Just as we pray for each other, and in this way share in Christ's mediation, so our priests act in the person of Christ, as he has given the Church the authority to do so: go – teach, heal, forgive sins.... Mary is given the title of Mediatrix because of her

---

15 Quoted in Trevor Willis, *Can the Jehovah's Witnesses Survive?* (Kindle edition), location 2359.

unique role in giving Jesus her Son to us, and because of her role in praying for all her children.

Basic to Watchtower teachings is its rejection of the divinity of Christ, although to an extent it was not always so. *The Watchtower* magazine (3-1880, p. 83) said that 'To worship Christ in any form cannot be wrong', implying that at the beginning Russell accepted the divinity of Christ. In his book, 'Salvation' published by the Watchtower Society, Rutherford wrote:

> Christ Jesus is the "Everlasting Father", or "Life-giver". (Isaiah 9:6), (p. 179)
> Christ Jesus, the Divine.... (p. 195)
> Long before the coming of Christ Jesus to earth as a man God... (p. 200)

However, for most of the Watchtower's short history, it has emphatically denied the divinity of Christ.

There is a profound difference between the Catholic and the Watchtower approach to understanding the nature and person of Jesus Christ, and perhaps it can be summed up in the question, does the title 'Son of God' mean that Jesus was divine or not, that is, is he God the Son? The Catholic Faith says, yes, the Watchtower says, no.

Son of God

The Watchtower rightly points out, and Jesus himself makes the same point to the Jews when they objected to him using the term, Son of God, for himself (cf. John 10:34ff), that the title was often used as a title of honour, with no hint of divinity, and it is also used of Adam (Luke 3:38). It was given to kings and judges (cf. Psalm 82:1-6; Psalm 58:1). The Watchtower therefore says that this is the sense in which it must be applied to Jesus himself.

Is this how Jesus used the title for himself, or did he give it a far deeper meaning? One clue is that Jesus often simply calls himself the Son, without qualification. This is his relationship with his Father. The Watchtower does not mind calling Jesus the only-begotten son of God, because it immediately qualifies it by saying that this means he is the first of God's created beings, regardless of the fact that to be begotten does not mean to be created by the begetter. I pointed out to a Jehovah's Witness that no father begets a son who is different in nature to himself, but this was immediately rejected, although he was not able to give any instance to the contrary.

Because the Watchtower is adamant from the start that Jesus is not divine it therefore concentrates on those texts that imply that Jesus is inferior to his Father and it has various ways to deal with those passages that reveal his divinity. It mistranslates texts, ignores them, states baldly that the text cannot mean what it says or so whittles them away with sophistry that they become meaningless.

To be fair to the Watchtower, many texts, on a surface reading, do seem to imply an inferiority of Jesus to the Father, so it is important to have a look at these texts, see what the Watchtower says of them, and what the Catholic response is.

Equal to God and subject to him

The first thing to say is that the Catholic approach has always been, from the very beginning, to take seriously *all* that is said of Jesus, in his humanity and in his divinity, and seek to understand the fullness of what the Scriptures reveal to us. The first three centuries of the Christian Church was a period in which the Church came, through challenge and controversy, to an ever deeper and firmer understanding of her divine Lord. She meditated on those texts that showed Jesus weak, vulnerable, obedient to his Father, subject to him, and understood the full humanity of Jesus. Then, she also meditated on those texts that showed him claiming equality to his Father, even using for himself the Name of God, I AM, claiming for himself the attributes and prerogatives of God, and understood his full divinity. Both are true.

The hymn in Philippians 2:5-11 is a very important text, so we need to see what the Watchtower says of it. It renders verse 6 as

> although he was existing in God's form,
> gave no consideration to a seizure, namely,
> that he should be equal to God.

Its commentary says 'Verse 5 counsels Christians to imitate Christ in the matter here being discussed. Could they be urged to consider it 'not robbery' but their right, to 'be equal with God'? Surely not!' (*Reasoning from the Scriptures,* pp. 419, 420*).* Putting aside the clumsiness of the NWT rendering and the fact that the Watchtower does not explain how one can exist in God's form without being God, it is difficult to understand its reasoning. St Paul is urging Christians to have the same *humility* as Christ, who being God, did not cling to his equality with God, his Father, but emptied himself. There would be no humility in not clinging on to his divine form, or seizing something, if it did not belong to him by right.

Also, there are two Greek words in the passage translated as 'form – '*morphe*' and '*schema*'. *Morphe* is stronger than *schema*, denoting an outer form which gives precise expression to the inner reality, and it is *morphe* which is used in verse 6 – 'though he was in the *morphe* – the precise expression and inner reality - of God'.

The Watchtower renders verse 9 as 'God exalted him to a superior position', but in the Greek there is no mention of 'a superior position'. The Greek is *huperupsosen*, - highly exalted. It then advises the Jehovah's Witness: 'To help the person reason on that scripture, we might ask: "If Jesus was equal to God before he died and God later exalted him to a higher position, would that not put Jesus above God? Yet, how could anyone become superior to God?" Since the text does not say that the Father exalted him 'to a higher position' then its reasoning is spurious and has no bearing on the divine nature of Jesus. When the hymn says that God 'highly exalted' Jesus, it was contrasting the humiliation of his death on the Cross and his subsequent Resurrection and Ascension to his Father's right hand.

There is an intriguing passage in John 5:37 – 38 in which Jesus says, 'Moreover, the Father who sent me has testified on my behalf. But you have never heard his voice nor seen his form, and you do not have his word remaining in you, because you do not believe in the one whom he has sent.' The implication surely is that if the Jehovah's Witnesses had believed in the one whom the Father had sent then they would have heard the voice of God and seen his form; they would have his word abiding in them, because he who has seen Jesus has seen the Father (John 14:9).

I Corinthians 15:28

When everything is subjected to him, then the Son himself will [also] be subjected to him.'

This is a text that seems to support the Watchtower position, for how can Jesus be equal to the Father if he is subject to him? Once again, it is the difference between nature and function. The NAB explanation is that 'the

Father is the ultimate agent in the drama, and the final end of the process, to whom the Son and everything else is ordered.' Jesus subjects himself willingly to the Father's plan of salvation; the text says nothing of the divine nature he shares with his Father.

Nature and function

Some points need to be made here. The Watchtower, because it does not believe in the divinity of Christ, cannot understand the distinction between the nature of Jesus, *who* he is in himself, and his function, as it were, in relation to his Father within the life of the Trinity; this is at the heart of the Watchtower's confusion. To give a simple example, a father and son work together in a company. They are equal in sharing the same nature as humans, but their functions within the company will be different, although working for the same ends within the company. So the Father is the Creator, creating all things through the Son. The Son, and not the Father or the Holy Spirit, is the One who dies on the Cross. It is the Holy Spirit who is poured out on believers, who is the Spirit of both the Father and the Son.

Now, let us look at some of the texts that show Jesus in his humanity, which the Watchtower claims prove that Jesus was not divine.

The humanity of Christ

> Colossians 1:15-17
>
> He [Jesus] is the image of the invisible God, the firstborn of all creation. For in him were created all things in heaven and on earth, the visible and invisible, whether

> thrones or dominations or principalities or powers; all things were created through him and for him. He is before all things, and in him all things hold together.

This is a favourite text of the Watchtower to try and refute the divinity of Christ. One Watchtower commentary reads:

> Jesus is Jehovah's most precious Son – and for good reason. He is called 'the firstborn of all creation,' for he was God's first creation. There is something else that makes this Son special. He is the 'only-begotten Son' (John 3:16). This means that Jesus is the only one directly created by God. Jesus is also the only one whom God used when he created all other things.
> *What Does the Bible Really Teach?* p. 41

In the Watchtower understanding, the rest of creation differed from the created Son, because after being created the Son then co-operated with God in the act of the creating all other things. To make this clear, the Watchtower then inserts, totally gratuitously, and in contradiction to the Greek text, the word 'other', that is, 'were created all [other] things in heaven and on earth' citing examples when such a meaning is given elsewhere, for example, Luke 13:2, 21:29. However, it all depends on context and prior belief. The NWT version corresponds to Watchtower belief, the Catholic translation never includes the word 'other' because Jesus is begotten, not created, and it is not in the original Greek.

The First-born Son

Jesus is described as the First-born, and in the Scriptures this term is used in two ways. It can be used in the direct way of being the first-born from a woman, for example, Luke 2:7 'and she gave birth to her first-born son' (NB. In Hebrew usage this does not mean that there were sons after that). The second way is that of pre-eminence, rank or dignity, for example, in Exodus 4:22 Israel is described as 'my son, my first-born.' In Jeremiah 31:8 God says 'Ephraim is my first-born'.

In what way is the term used in Colossians 1? Paul himself gives the answer – 'For [that is, because] in him were created all things.' He is not referring here to the nature of Jesus as the First-born Son of God, the only-begotten Son, but to his pre-eminence before created things. It does not say that Jesus was created – he was begotten, and 'in him' all things were created.

John 17:3

> Now this is eternal life, that they should know you, the only true God, and the one you have sent, Jesus Christ.

The Watchtower (*Reasoning From Scripture,* p. 212) asks us to note 'that Jesus referred not to himself but to his Father in heaven as "the only true God" '.

This verse is a later editorial gloss on the two preceding verses, for Jesus nowhere refers to himself as Jesus Christ. Here, Jesus is praying that his Father will give him the glory that he himself has, and which Jesus possessed before the world began. In Isiaih 42:8 and 48:11 God says he 'will not yield his glory to another' so the glory Jesus has is intrinsic to his divine nature and he prays that he will receive that glory in his human nature, too The context makes it clear that Jesus is conscious of his own unique relationship with his Father, and that he wants his coming death to glorify his Father. It is not referring to his divine nature.

A Jehovah's Witness will often refer to the fact that Jesus prays to his Father, as in this instance, and say, 'How can God pray to God?' Of course, in these passages we are given a precious glimpse into the very dialogue of love within the Trinity Itself, an eternal love dialogue of God the Father speaking to God the Son, a sharing of love who is the Holy Spirit, now made visible, in Jesus' communing with his Father, on earth. Jesus is not praying to himself but to his Father.

John 20:17
This passage recounts the incident in the garden when Mary Magdalene meets Jesus; He tells her not to cling to him, because 'I have not yet ascended to My Father and Your Father, to My God and your God.'

The Watchtower comments (*Reasoning From the Scriptures,* p. 212), 'So to the resurrected Jesus, the Father was God, just as the Father was God to Mary Magdalene.'

Quite so. Catholics would never deny that the Father is God, and equally that Jesus is his Son. But Jesus is making a distinction between his relationship with the Father and the Father's relationship with Mary Magdalen; we, too, have that relationship with our heavenly Father. Jesus is using Hebrew parallelism, where the same statement is said in two different ways. Jesus is not denying his divine status as Son. Also, in the New Testament, the word God is used when the Father is meant, but this never denies the divinity of Christ.

The divinity of Christ in the New Testament

John 1:1. The Word was God.
This is perhaps the most contentious text for the Watchtower, and it goes to great lengths to blur the obvious meaning of the Greek.

In *Reasoning From the Scriptures,* p. 212 it first lists versions of the text from different Bibles, some, including the Jerusalem Bible, which gives the translation 'and the Word was God'. Others, such as Moffatt and Schonfield, translate it as 'the Word /Logos was divine'. Then, that the NWT and the Emphatic Diaglot, which the Watchtower uses as its preferred Greek/English text, render it as 'the Word was a god' and 'a god was the Word', respectively. The Watchtower then poses the question, 'What is it that these translators are seeing in the Greek text that moves some of them to refrain from saying "the Word was God" '? Its explanation is, put rather more simply than *Reasoning From the Scriptures,* that the noun, [God], without an article, points to a quality about someone, whereas the noun, Word, with the article, points to an identity, a personality. 'So the text is not saying that the Word (Jesus) was the same as the God with whom *he was,* but, rather, that the Word was godlike, divine, a god'.

Is the Watchtower's grammatical explanation of the text correct, though?

The Word was God

Theos en ho logos (John 1:1) – as every genuine Greek scholar will tell us, grammatically this can be translated only as 'the Word was God'. The Greek rule is that the predicate (what is said about the subject; that is, what is said about the Word, subject of the sentence) is that the Word is God (describes what is). A predicate noun or adjective seldom has the article. No genuine Greek scholar would translate it as 'the word was a god'. That the Watchtower accepts the Greek scholars' grammar when it suits it is confirmed when it translates correctly such texts as, for example John 5:27, 9:5, and 1.18 which have the same construct at John 1:1. If the Watchtower was consistent it would translate these texts as 'he is a son of man', I am a light of the world, 'no man has ever seen a god'.

Matthew 11:27
No one knows the Son except the Father, just as no one knows the Father except the Son and those to whom the Son chooses to reveal him.

To 'know' someone in the Scriptures has a far deeper meaning than even the knowing we have of close friends; it is the intimacy of union, of the deepest relationship possible. Even though we cannot know God from our own human perspective, it is Jesus who reveals the Father to us so that we can enter into that intimacy with him.

John 1:18
'No one has ever seen God. The only Son, God, who is at the Father's side, has revealed him.'

The commentary of the *NAB for Catholics* says, "While the vast majority of later textual witnesses have another reading, 'the Son, the only one' or 'the only Son', the translation above follows the best and earliest manuscripts, *mongenēs theos,* but takes the first term to mean not just 'Only One' but to include a filial relationship with the Father, as at Luke 9:38 (only child) or Hebrews 11:17, 'only son' and as translated in John 1:14. The Logos is thus 'only son' and God but not Father/God.'"

One Witness said that Jesus had to be less than God the Father because he is the Son and the son always comes after the father in time. This, of course, is spurious, because time did not exist before God created the universe. In eternity there is no time. There never was a time when God the Father was not Father, and therefore there was no point at which Jesus was not Son, co-equal and co-eternal with the Father.

The Watchtower points to this verse as confirming that Jesus was not God because it says that no one has ever seen God. 'Had any human seen Jesus Christ, the Son? Of course! So, then, was John saying that Jesus was God? Obviously not.' (*ibid.*, p. 213) However, as we saw above, to be consistent it would have to translate the text as 'no man has ever seen a god', which negates its argument, since it teaches that Jesus was 'a god'.

Also, John was affirming that Jesus was saying that no-one has seen God the Father in his divine nature, but we do see him veiled within the human nature of Jesus Christ, for 'he who has seen me sees the Father' (John 14:9); Jesus also affirms that by seeing him 'henceforth you know him and have seen him' (v.7).

Matthew 26:63-66
Jesus is asked directly by the High Priest: 'I put you on oath by the living God to tell us if you are the Christ [Messiah] Son of God'. Jesus answers in the affirmative but goes further. He draws on the vision of the Son of Man in Daniel 7:13: 'You will see the Son of Man seated at the right hand of the Power [equivalent to the sacred name of God] and coming on the clouds of heaven'. He is here saying he is more than the Messiah. He is equal to God and the High Priest understands this. He tears his clothes saying, 'You have heard the blasphemy' to which all reply, 'He deserves to die'.

There are several texts that point directly to the divinity of Christ:

Isaiah 6:1-6: see John 12:41 (36-41). Isaiah saw the glory of YHWH enthroned in the heavenly temple, but John said that it was Jesus Isaiah saw, even then the visible manifestation of the invisible God.

Hebrews 1:8
"But of the Son: 'Your throne, O God, stands forever and ever.' (Quoting Psalm: 45:7). An alternative translation, given as a footnote in many Bibles, and used as the Watchtower text in the NWT, is 'God is your throne forever.' However, I am at a loss to know how anyone could explain how God could be anyone's throne, and how God could be the throne of Jesus. The author of Hebrews shows that he intended the text to demonstrate the divinity of Christ because he goes on to quote, in verses 10-12 Psalm 102: 26-28, which is addressed to God and applied here to Jesus.

'The Father and I are one.' John 10:30
'*hen*', 'one', is the neuter form, meaning one reality. The most accurate translation is 'My Father and I are one being.'

Pointing to this verse, a Jehovah's Witness quoted John 17:21 to me, 'in order that they may all be one, just as you, Father, are in union with me and I am in union with you, that they also may be in union with us.'(NWT). (The Watchtower consistently renders '*en*' as 'in union with' rather the more accurate translation 'in', which points to a much more profound reality, both within God himself and the relationship we have with the Trinity). The Witness pointed to the manifest disunity among Christians and asked how this verse could possibly point to the oneness we claim for the Father, Son and Holy Spirit. Of course, that is looking at it through the wrong end of the telescope. The union, the oneness within the Trinity is the reality, the paradigm, towards which we as Christians should be aiming for, both visibly with each other and with each Christian's union with God, being 'in' him. Even so, the union called for - 'so that they may be one' - is not the same oneness as in John 10.30, because it is a prayer, not a statement of fact.

Colossians 2:9
'For in him dwells the whole fullness of the deity/godhead bodily.'

The Watchtower NWT 'translates it as 'divine quality', thus changing the Greek from *'theotetos'* 'Godhead' to *'theotes'*, 'divine quality'. *Theotetos* can never be translated as divine quality. It means divinity, deity, divine nature, not divine quality.

John 5:18
'For this reason the Jews tried all the more to kill him, because he not only broke the Sabbath but he also called God his own Father, making himself equal to God.'

Again, no son can have a nature different to that of his father, as the Jews here are acknowledging. They knew exactly what Jesus was claiming. In the previous verse 17, Jesus says, 'My Father is at work until now, so I am at work.' The NAB commentary is: 'Jesus here claims the same authority to work as the Father, and in the discourse that follows, the same divine prerogative power over life and death and judgement.'

The Jews obviously understood that Jesus was indeed claiming equality with God, because they took up stones to kill him for blasphemy.

John 20:28
'Thomas answered him, 'My Lord and my God.'

One Jehovah's Witness said that when Thomas was saying 'My Lord' he was looking at Jesus, but when he said 'my God' he was looking upwards to heaven. Of course, I'm not sure how he knew this, as he was not there at the time! The Watchtower (*Reasoning From the Scriptures,* p. 213) refers back to its interpretation of John 1:1 'and the Word was a god' to explain this verse. It has no problem describing Jesus as a 'god' while vehemently denying that Jehovah's Witnesses are polytheists, without giving an explanation as to how they can believe in God and another god or gods, when there is only one God.

Other texts show Jesus taking to himself titles that the Scriptures reserve to God alone:

Revelation 1:8, 22:13.
I am the Alpha and the Omega.

Jesus applies to himself words used by God to describe himself. See Isaiah 44:6 – 'I am the first and I am the last (that is, in Greek Alpha and Omega); there is no God but me.'

John 8:58
Before Abraham came to be, I AM – *ego eimi*.

This can only be translated as 'I am', not 'I am he' as the NWT does. This is the name of God revealed to Moses at the burning bush in its Greek form (Exodus 3:14).

The NWT renders Exodus 3:14 as 'I shall prove to be what I shall prove to be', and 'I shall prove to be has sent me to you.' It is strange that in the very text where God reveals his divine name which the Watchtower renders as Jehovah, it does not use it, instead using one possible meaning for it.

It renders John 8:58 as 'Before Abraham came into existence, I have been.' Of course, *'ego eimi'* is in the present tense not the past tense.

2 Corinthians 5:19
God was in Christ reconciling the world to himself.

'In Christ' is one of St Paul's favourite expressions, but the Watchtower consistently renders it in other ways, which diminishes Jesus' role in our salvation. This text becomes 'Namely that God was by means of Christ reconciling the world to himself', and John 1:4: 'All that came to be had life in him and that light was the light of men' becomes 'By means of him was life, and the life was the life of men'. So Jesus in the Watchtower dispensation is no longer the Light of the world or the Way, the Truth and the Life.

Revelation 22:3
The throne of God and of the Lamb.
One throne, therefore one rule.

Matthew 28:19
Go, therefore, and make disciples of all nations, baptizing them in the name of the Father, and of the Son, and of the Holy Spirit.

As we have seen, the name, in Hebrew thought, expresses a person's being. The name, YHWH, was revealed to Moses in the Old Testament. In the New Testament Jesus now reveals the inner reality of that Name: it is Father, Son and Holy Spirit. This reveals God's nature and being.

At one visit by a Jehovah's Witness I got him to acknowledge that the Name of God expresses the nature of God himself, and that there is only one Name by which he is called. When I pointed out that in this verse the one

Name of God is given as Father, Son and Holy Spirit, he was silent for a moment then jumped up saying, 'I can never believe that' and hurried out of the house, with his companion scurrying after him.

Not an angel:

Hebrews 1:4
Far superior to the angels.
Verse 5 - For to which of the angels did God ever say: 'You are my son; this day I have begotten you?'

The text in Hebrews then goes on to apply Scriptures, Psalm 45:8 and Psalm 102: 26-28, addressed to God in the Old Testament but now applied to Jesus.

As to the Watchtower belief that Jesus is an angel, see below for a discussion about this.

Jesus did things reserved to God alone:

Jesus revealed his divine nature, not only in words, but also by the things he did., taking on himself acts and actions that belonged to God alone.

Mark 2:7
Who can forgive sins but God alone?

Jesus is taking to himself the power to forgive sins, which the Pharisees knew was blasphemy, since the forgiveness of sins is reserved to God alone. In the New Testament, Jesus, who as God has authority to forgive sins, passes that authority on to the apostles and therefore to their successors (John 20:22, 23) and which we receive in the Sacrament of Confession/Reconciliation. Of course, we are all commanded to forgive those who sin against us, but only God has the power to forgive that person's sins.

Mark 2:27
The Son of Man is master even of the Sabbath.
The holy day of the Sabbath was given to the Jews by God himself. Just as God 'rested', ceased from work, on the seventh day, so his people were cease from work on the Sabbath. Jesus was declaring himself equal to God by saying he was master of the Sabbath.

Very early on, the Church began to celebrate the day of the new creation when Jesus rose from the dead on the eighth day, the Lord's Day (Acts 20:7). 'This would begin on the Saturday evening, because the day was reckoned in the Jewish fashion.' (JB note k), from six o'clock in the evening to six o'clock in the evening of the following day. This is why the Church celebrates evening Masses on Saturdays, for Sundays and Holy Days.

Matthew 14:22-33.
Jesus walks on water.
Pagan gods were often depicted sitting on dry land with the waters above and the waters below, which was also the underworld of the dead of which they were the masters. But to God alone is the power to control the wind and the waves, the elements of nature. The disciples acknowledged Jesus had this power when they bowed down before him, declaring 'Truly, you are the Son of God, (v.33)

Note that when Jesus healed people, gave sight to the blind, gave the deaf hearing, raised the dead, he did all these things by his own power (cf Luke 8:46). He did not invoke his Father, but knew he was carrying out the Father's will on earth.

Testimony of the Early Church

Christians have consistently understood these and other texts as affirming the divinity of Christ, but the Watchtower asserts that as soon as the last apostle had died, the Church slipped into pagan apostasy by making Jesus God.

Did St John, for example, in his Gospel (John 1:1) really intend this to affirm the divinity of Christ, or has the Church misunderstood him all these centuries? Surely the ones to know best the mind of St John would be his disciples, those who had learnt their faith from his own lips. As we have seen, such a one was St Ignatius of Antioch, and here are just a few quotations from the letters he wrote to various Christian communities on his way to Rome and martyrdom:

> We shall be his (Jesus') temples, and he will be within us as our God – as he actually is.
>
> The source of your unity and election is genuine suffering which you undergo by the will of the Father and of Jesus Christ our God. *Ephesians 1.*
>
> He encouraged them to be 'imitators of God, and having your hearts kindled in the blood of God.' (*ibid*).
>
> For our God, Jesus Christ, who was conceived in the womb by Mary (*ibid., 18*).
>
> God appeared in the likeness of man unto newness of everlasting life (*ibid., 19*).
>
> Ignatius...to the church that is beloved and enlightened through the will of Him who willed all things that exist, by faith

and love towards Jesus Christ our God. (*Roman 1*).

It was only in the 4th Century that Arius challenged this belief and denied the divinity of Christ. As we have seen, under this attack the Church was impelled to examine her beliefs and reaffirm her belief in Jesus Christ, God from God, Light from light, True God from true God, begotten not made, one in substance with the Father.

The main reason why the Watchtower rejects the divinity of Christ is that it is unable to distinguish between his eternal being, one nature with God his Father, and his human nature which he took on as man.

Jesus Christ according to the Watchtower

If the Watchtower does not share the orthodox Christian belief in Jesus Christ as true God and true man, the only-begotten Son of God, what does it teach its followers about him?

Pre-existent Spirit

It teaches that Jesus had a pre-existence in heaven before he came on earth as man, but as 'a spirit creature' the first one to be created by God and 'the only one directly created by God' (*What does the Bible Really Teach?* p. 41) – because God then used him to create all other things. In this, the Watchtower is referring to Colossians 1:15:16. As we have already seen, while it is correct in acknowledging that all things were created through him, it is wrong when it asserts that Jesus also was created 'in his pre-human existence'. Rather, his pre-eminence as first-born is because all things were created in him, through him and for him[16], not that he himself was created.

Michael the Archangel=Jesus?

One of the most baffling Watchtower doctrines is that Jesus was Michael the Archangel before his birth as Jesus, and reverted to being Michael after his reconstitution as a spirit being following his death.

Its main text for this is 1 Thessalonians 4:16:

> For the Lord himself, with a word of command, with the voice of an archangel and with the trumpet of God, will come down from heaven. And the dead in Christ will rise first.

The Watchtower comment on this is:

> 'The command of Jesus Christ for the resurrection to begin is described as "the archangel's call" and Jude 9 says that the archangel is Michael. Would it be

---

[16] At one visit the Witness asked me why God created the world. I replied that it was created for Jesus, as in Colossians 1:16. The Witness brushed this aside in favour of what is for them the primary purpose, that the world was created for us human beings, but which is for Christians the secondary purpose. The world was given to us to care for it, but that is different than being created for our sake. This is an example of how the Watchtower teaches the Witnesses to brush aside Scripture in favour of its own preconceptions. How much richer the Witnesses' spiritual life would be if they could meditate on the truth that the whole of creation was created for Jesus Christ!

appropriate to liken Jesus' commanding call to that of someone of lesser authority? Reasonably, then, the archangel Michael is Jesus Christ.
Reasoning from the Scriptures, p. 218

There is absolutely no warrant in these texts to identify Jesus as Michael the archangel. The text is talking of the sound of a voice only, not Michael himself, while the Watchtower does not identify Jesus as also being a trumpet! Rather, the command, the voice, the sound of the trumpet, accompanies Jesus as he comes down from heaven.

The second text it uses is Revelation 12: 7-12:

> Then war broke out in heaven; Michael and his angels battled against the dragon. The dragon and its angels fought back, but they did not prevail and there was no longer any place for them in heaven. The huge dragon, the ancient serpent, who is called the Devil and Satan, who deceived the whole world, was thrown down to earth, and its angels were thrown down with it.

The Watchtower commentary says that:

> Michael and his angels would war against Satan and hurl him and his wicked angels out of heaven in connection with the conferring of kingly authority on Christ. Jesus is later depicted as leading the armies of heaven in war against the nations of the world (Rev. 19:11-16). Is it not reasonable that Jesus would also be the one to take

action against the one he described as 'ruler of this world', Satan the Devil? (John 12:31) Daniel 12:1 associates the 'standing up of Michael' to act with the authority with 'a time of trouble, such as never has been since there was a nation till that time.' That would certainly fit the experience of the nations when Christ as heavenly executioner takes action against them. So the evidence indicates that the Son of God was known as Michael before he came to earth and is known also by that name since his return to heaven where he resides as the glorified spirit Son of God (*ibid.*).

Note that these none of the texts used by the Watchtower equate Jesus with Michael; note also the use of the word 'reasonable'. Speculation, human reasoning, has become for the Watchtower a set doctrine. Everything the Watchtower turns to is supposition, that it is 'reasonable' and then hardens this supposition into 'fact'. It should be sufficient to accept Hebrews 1:5-14, which specifically denies that Jesus is an angel, to refute the Watchtower belief. It simply ignores this text, despite saying that the organisation bases all its beliefs on the Bible. I have quoted the text from Hebrews to them time and time again, but am always met with silence.

It is interesting that, in its publications, the Watchtower continues to speak of the Son of God as Jesus, not Michael, when discussing his existence before becoming Man, and his post-Resurrection being, so the suspicion is that for all practical purposes the Witnesses have to follow this 'new light' and adhere in principle to the doctrine, while simply ignoring it in reality.

There are some other teachings that need to be explored in greater depth:

> That he was crucified on a stake, not a cross, and was resurrected back to spirit life not to risen life, then does not receive his kingly power until 1914.

These teachings will be discussed in detail in later chapters.

Kingly power

'There, he "sat down at the right hand of God" and waited to receive kingly power – Hebrews 10:12,13.' (*What does the Bible Really Teach?* p. 46). We need to read the actual text of these two verses from Hebrews, because they do not say what the Watchtower implies they do:

> ... and took his seat forever at the right hand of God; now he waits until his enemies are made his footstool.

In Chapter 19 we shall see why the Watchtower says that Jesus was waiting, not until his enemies are made his footstool, but to receive kingly power.

The Ransom Sacrifice of Jesus

The Watchtower mostly follows orthodox Christian, Scriptural teaching in its explanation of Jesus' sacrifice of himself as ransoming us from sin and death. Because Jesus was sinless, he could offer himself freely to his Father as a ransom, redeeming us from the penalty of death incurred by Adam's sin and enabling us to live a life pleasing to God.

However, orthodox Christianity has gone further than this and said that the 'perfect human life' of Jesus, in the Watchtower words, would not be sufficient for the fullness of his expiation for sin. Because God is infinite, then the offence done to him by sin is infinite (cf Mark 3:28-30); it could not be expiated by finite man. Therefore only God himself, in the divine person of Jesus, could offer that infinite expiation. On the other hand, since sin was committed by man, then only a human being could expiate the offence, so the Word became man to offer the perfect sacrifice on our behalf.

When it comes to what Jesus has subsequently won for us by his death, then the Watchtower parts company with the Scriptures into its own beliefs, which distinguishes 144,000 who share a life in Heaven with Jesus, and the 'great crowd' who will live forever in a paradise on earth. These two Watchtower doctrines will be examined in subsequent chapters.

CHAPTER 8

THE HOLY SPIRIT

The 1/10/2010 issue of *The Watchtower* was devoted to a discussion about the Holy Spirit, and the way the Watchtower handles the subject gives us some idea of how to assess its approach to the Scriptures; we can then see how to approach the arguments it uses. The issue seemed to be directed specifically towards Catholics – which is probably why the Jehovah's Witnesses came round especially to give me a copy!

It begins by quoting the Holy Father, Pope Benedict XV1 in an address he gave in Australia: 'A clear understanding of the Spirit almost seems beyond our reach,' as if this should make us uneasy. Yes, of course, a clear understanding is almost beyond our reach because as we have seen, God is not limited to the bounds of human thought and reason; on the other hand, Pope Benedict says 'almost', because God himself has come down on earth in Jesus and dwells within us to reveal something of his being to us, so we *can* understand something of the Holy Spirit, since he is living within us.

The article lists some replies it had received to the question of 'What is the holy spirit?'

A real person who lives inside Christ's disciples,
Divine science, a law of God in action,
God's presence at work in the world,
The third person of the Trinity.

Then, the Watchtower asks, 'Why such confusion?' There is not necessarily any confusion, because the Holy Spirit cannot be limited to one answer. Its answer is that 'It dates back to the fourth century C.E. when some theologians claimed that the holy spirit was a person who was somehow equal to God.' It then quotes from the *New Catholic Encyclopaedia*:

> 'The Old Testament clearly does not envisage God's spirit as a person.... God's spirit is simply God's power'. The same source adds: 'The majority of New Testament texts reveal God's spirit as something, not someone; this is especially seen in the parallelism between the spirit and the power of God.'

It is difficult so assess the accuracy of these quotations; I have read the article on the Holy Spirit in the *Catholic Encyclopaedia*[17] and failed to find the above quotation. It is true that the Old Testament 'does not envisage God's spirit as a person' because the revelation of God's being as Triune was not fully revealed before Christ's coming. The second quotation in no way represents Catholic teaching, and never has. Bear in mind that the Watchtower does misrepresent its quotations and cannot be relied on to give

---

[17] Available on line. The article is listed under 'Holy Ghost', and gives a full treatment of the Catholic understanding of the Holy Spirit.

an accurate representation. Instead, we need to examine what the Church really teaches.

The Holy Spirit as Person

The Watchtower defines the Holy Spirit as God's active force that executes his will, who is not a Person, nor the Third Person of the Blessed Trinity.

> A comparison of Bible texts that refer to the holy spirit shows that it is spoken of as 'filling' people; they can be 'baptized' with it; they can be 'anointed' with it. (Luke 1:41; Matt: 3:11; Acts 10:38) None of these expressions would be appropriate if the holy spirit were a person
> *Reasoning From the Scriptures,* p. 380

The quote above, with some saying 'A real person who lives inside Christ's disciples', shows that people misunderstand what Christian theology understands by 'person'. To put it simply, 'person' is *who* we are, 'nature is *what* we are.

> Every creature, therefore, that possesses an intelligent nature is a person. Every angel is a person; every human being – even the unborn child or one who is insane – is a person. Once the intelligent nature exists, the person exists.[18]

---

[18] Michael Sheehan: *Apologetics and Catholic Doctrine,* (London, The Saint Austin Press, 2001), pp. 311-312.

So we do not mean 'person' as 'a human being', although a human being is a person. In *What the Bible Really Teaches,* p.160, the Watchtower acknowledges that 'By learning about him [God] through the pages of the Bible, however, you can come to know him as a person.'

Because the Holy Spirit is an intelligent nature, by his very nature as Spirit he can truly fill us, we can be anointed and baptized in him, because that is true to his nature.

The Scriptures show him exhibiting the characteristics of an intelligent nature:

We can grieve God's Holy Spirit. When Ananias and Sapphira lied, they are told that 'You lied to the Holy Spirit. You have lied not to human beings, but to God' (Acts 5:1-4), equating the Holy Spirit with God.

He is given to us as Comforter and Helper. (John 16:7) When Jesus breathed on the disciples he gave them the Holy Spirit (John 20:32); that is, he bequeathed to us his own Spirit, who cannot be less than himself. (In this instance Jesus is bestowing the Holy Spirit on the disciples with the authority to forgive sins in his name, which is passed on to their successors in the sacrament of confession/reconciliation).

He prays within us (Romans 8:26, 27, Galatians 4:6). How can an impersonal force pray within us or utter the word 'Abba', unless the Holy Spirit, who is also the spirit of Jesus himself, utters that expression of Jesus' own relationship with his Father?

'The fruits of the Spirit are love, joy, peace, patience, kindness, generosity, faithfulness, gentleness, self-control' (Galatians 5:22, 23). These are not the attributes of an impersonal force, which could never instil such qualities within a human being; they are the attributes of a personal being. In fact, because the Holy Spirit proceeds from the Father and the Son he instils the love of God within us as manifested in these attributes. The Holy Spirit is the Spirit of Love between the Father and the Son. Since he is God's very nature, then he cannot be less than God.

Personification

The Watchtower counters these texts by saying, rightly, that the Scriptures sometimes personifies things, for example, sin (Genesis 4:7, 8), and wisdom (Proverbs 8). However, this does not mean that this applies in the case of the Holy Spirit. The Scriptures show unequivocally that the Holy Spirit truly does intercede for us, acts as our Comforter and Advocate, prays in us, is truly grieved, infuses the virtues. These are not figures of speech or the personification of an abstract entity but the attributes of personhood.

The Watchtower also points out that the Holy Spirit is given impersonal names – dove, water, wind, breath, and therefore he cannot be person. However, Jesus himself is sometimes described in impersonal terms – Lion of Judah, Lamb of God, Alpha and Omega, Morning Star, etc., and God is also given impersonal names such as Rock and Fortress, Shield, so this objection does not stand.

Jesus himself speaks of the Holy Spirit in personal terms:

> [W]hen he comes, the Spirit of Truth, he will guide you to all truth. He will not speak on his own, but he will speak what he hears, and he will declare to you the things that are coming. He will glorify me, because he will take from what is mine and declare it to you (John 16:13, 14).

If the Holy Spirit was an impersonal force as the Watchtower teaches, not Person, he could do none of this.

These verses need to be pondered deeply, because they also give us an insight into the depths and relationship within the Most Blessed Trinity, where each Person listens, receives, gives, speaks, glorifies.

Ironically, as we shall see when discussing the Resurrection, the Watchtower has no difficulty in seeing the Risen Jesus, in its terms a 'Spirit Being', as a manifestation in visible form, yet cannot see that the Holy Spirit can be manifested in *the forms of* a dove, fire, wind. Notice that the Scriptures do not say the Holy Spirit *is* a dove, fire, wind, etc. but appeared in those forms.

CHAPTER 9

CROSS OR TORTURE STAKE

A distinctive Watchtower teaching is its rejection of the Cross as the instrument on which Jesus died, in favour of a 'torture stake'. In fact, it was only in the 1930s that Joseph Rutherford, who in 1916 succeeded Russell as President of the Watchtower Society, decided that Jesus died on a stake rather than a cross. Before that, Watchtower publications showed Jesus crucified in the traditional way.

The Watchtower rightly points out that the Greek '*stauros*' means an upright stake, an upright pole. This is because there is no word in Greek for 'cross' so *stauros* was used by Greek-speaking Christians when describing the Cross on which Jesus died. It was the Romans who devised this method of torture and death, not the Greeks. The Scriptures also talk of the tree and the wood of the cross, which we often use in our liturgy; for example, during the Good Friday liturgy we proclaim, 'Behold the wood of the Cross, on which our Redeemer hung, come let us adore.' When we use it in this way there is no thought whatever that this has to be a stake rather than a cross.

The main reason for this Watchtower belief is that it points to some pagan religions that have used the cross in their religion, for example in the Chaldean worship of Tammuz, or of Bacchus, Bel and Odin. It quotes the 1946 *Encyclopedia Britannica*, 'The use of the cross as a religious symbol of pre-Christian times and among non-Christian peoples may probably be regarded as almost universal, and in very many cases it was connected with some form of nature worship.'

Reasoning From the Scriptures, p. 90

If true, and there is some disagreement about this, it should not disturb a Catholic, because we could see this as God preparing the Gentile world for the redemptive death of his Only Begotten Son on the Cross. What the cross prefigured in pagan religions received its fulfilment on Calvary. The myth, in the words of C.S. Lewis, became reality.

What the Watchtower does not mention is that an upright stake is equally of pagan origin, as we can see today in standing stones, for example. The worship of Astarte, in the Middle East, also has an upright pole as its symbol, which is closer to the Holy Land than Odin.

Of course, the obvious fact is that Christians venerate the cross because it was the actual way in which Jesus died, not because of any previous symbolism.[19]

---

[19] As to veneration of relics of the True Cross, the accusation is often made that the relics would make several crosses. However, a French Scholar, Charles de Rohalt de Fleury has catalogued all existing relics and found they would not be enough to make one cross. Also, it is understandable if more than one type of wood is involved, for the upright, the pabulum and the notice pinned above Christ's head would probably all have come from different woods.

Idolatry?

The Watchtower then goes on to equate Catholic reverence of the Crucifix as idolatry, which of course is a travesty. We do not worship the Cross, but it is a reminder to us of the sacrifice and death that Jesus endured for us, and the redemption he has won for us.

To a certain extent, it is true that the representation of the cross does not often occur in the first century or two of the Christian Church. Crucifixion was still being used as a method of execution, including of Christians, and the full horror of it was literally in front of people's eyes. Another reason was that the early Christians were well aware that the symbol of the cross was used in other religions, and were often mocked for it, so were reluctant to use it publicly. They were aware of the difference between its significance for them and its significance in pagan use, and did not want to be associated with wrong use. Instead, they used euphemistic symbols such as the anchor or the sign of a fish, which in Greek (*ichthus*) is an acronym for 'Jesus Christ Son of God, Saviour'.

Nevertheless, recent discoveries have shown evidence that Christians very early on did use the symbol of the cross, although discreetly. A wall painting of the cross has been discovered in the ruins of Pompey: 1st century ossuaries, (boxes containing the bones of the dead) bearing the sign of the cross have been found in a cave near Bethany; a 1st century burial chamber with ossuaries has been uncovered on the Mount of Olives inscribed with the sign of the cross. A prayer room has also been discovered at Herculaneum, a cross representation showing that it was Christian. Christians were accustomed to signing themselves with the sign of the cross and Tertullian, by the year 200, was saying that Christians were wearing away their foreheads because of their custom of signing themselves with the sign of the cross before everything they did.

However, it was not until Queen Helena, the mother of Constantine, discovered the tomb of Christ and fragments of the True Cross in the fourth century, by which time crucifixion had been abolished, that Christians began to use it much more in the liturgy and in visual representation.

The Cross in Early Christian writings

In the writings of the Early Church Fathers there is evidence that they knew that Jesus died on a cross, not an upright stake. The Epistle of Barnabas speaks of 'the cross was to express the grace [of our redemption] by the letter T', and the Epistle, as well as Justin Martyr, Irenaeus, Tertullian and Minucius Felix all speak of people praying in the *orans,* praying, position, with arms outstretched in the form of a cross, symbolic of the one on which Jesus died. They drew especially on the image of Moses praying with arms outstretched, (Exodus 17:11) which they saw as prefiguring Christ on the Cross.

Can the Watchtower produce any evidence from the Early Fathers that early Christians actually drew on pagan religions for the Cross? No. Besides, when the Romans crucified Jesus, they were using their usual methods to execute a non- Roman criminal – they would certainly not be thinking of the Christian Church worshipping it as a pagan symbol in centuries to come!

What sort of Cross?

We now know much more about methods of Roman crucifixion than Joseph Rutherford did. Unless there were hundreds being crucified at once, along the road to Sephhoris, as for example, after an uprising such as took place when Jesus was twelve years old, the upright stake would be permanently in the ground at the place of execution. The condemned man would go to the place of execution carrying the pabulum or crossbeam, which is what Jesus did. The condemned man would then be fixed to the cross with nails, or rope, or both. There would sometimes be a stirrup that he could rest on, but this was intended to prolong his agony. The cross could be in the shape of a T or in the more familiar cross shape. Since the panel bearing Jesus' 'crimes' was fixed above his head, one can assume that his was the cross shape. The heel bone of a crucified man has been found, showing the nail driven through the heel, which means the legs could sometimes have been secured sideways.

Evidence in the New Testament

In R*easoning from Scriptures* (p. 89) there is a quotation from *The Non-Christian Cross* by J.D. Parsons (London 1896), who was a member of the Society for Psychical Research:

> There is not a single sentence in any of the numerous writings forming the New Testament, which, in the original Greek, bears even indirect evidence to the effect that the stauros used in the case of Jesus was other than an ordinary stauros; much less to the effect that it consisted, not of one piece of timber, but of two pieces nailed together in the form of a cross.

In this the author is wrong. In its books the Watchtower invariably shows Jesus 'impaled', as they term it, on a stake, with his hands fastened above his head with a single nail through his wrists, and one through his feet. This was an impossible position, in which the victim would die very quickly by asphyxiation within fifteen minutes, and not languish sometimes for several days or even for the three hours that Jesus hung on the Cross. In addition, when Jesus appeared to his disciples after his Resurrection, Thomas said, 'Unless I see the mark of the nails in his hands and put my finger into the nail marks.... I will not believe' (John 20:25). Thomas says *nails*, not *nail*, implying that Jesus had more than one nail in his hands, as he would have on a cross, not the one nail in Watchtower depictions. Living at the time, Thomas had undoubtedly seen how crucifixions were carried out. One Witness, when I pointed this out, simply dismissed it as irrelevant, but it isn't, because we are dealing here with historical fact, not myth, and such clues are vital.

Since J.D. Parsons wrote, and Joseph Rutherford formulated his opinions, there has been a great deal of research done on Roman crucifixion, and our knowledge has greatly increased.

Practical considerations

Further, there is a very practical consideration of it not being a 'torture stake'. If Jesus had been 'impaled' as the Watchtower asserts, it would have had to be a very long and heavy piece of wood indeed. It would have needed at least two feet or more to be set into the ground to provide a secure upright on which to hang a body. It would have needed at least another eight or nine feet to hang the body with the arms extended above the head and enough space left between the ground and the feet. Add another foot or so above the hands on which the indictment board was nailed, and the stake would have had to have been at least 12 feet long. It would have had to have been a substantial piece of wood, too, on which to support the dead weight of a body. Since Jesus 'carried his own cross', it seems doubtful that even a very strong and fit man would have been able to carry it, let alone a man who had been scourged and tortured. In fact, Jesus was relieved only of the *pabulum* and it was given to Simon of Cyrene after he had carried it some way.

Conclusion

Catholics do not worship the Cross. We venerate and honour it because it is the instrument on which Jesus won our redemption. Catholics love the Crucifix because it reminds us of the death Jesus died for us and the pains he bore for us and the extremity to which his immense love for us took him. We do not venerate it because it was a pagan symbol but because that was the way Jesus died, on a Cross, not impaled on a torture stake.

There is a further issue to explore. What did Jesus accomplish by his death on the Cross? This is what we shall investigate next.

CHAPTER 10

THE RANSOM SACRIFICE OF JESUS

The Watchtower rightly acknowledges the ransom sacrifice of Jesus. It defines 'ransom' as

> A price paid to buy back or to bring about release from some obligation or undesirable circumstance. The most significant ransom price is that of the shed blood of Jesus Christ. By paying over the value of that ransom in heaven, Jesus opened the way for Adam's offspring to be delivered from the sin and death that we all inherit because of the sin of our forefather Adam.
> *Reasoning From the Scriptures,*
> pp. 305, 306

This is in line with the Scriptures, for example I Peter 1:18-20, Romans 8:32. The *Catechism of the Catholic Church* puts it thus:

> The sacrifice of Christ is unique; it completes and surpasses all other sacrifices. First, it is a gift from God the Father himself, for the Father handed his Son over to sinners in order to reconcile us with himself. At the same time it is the offering of the Son of God made man, who in freedom and love offered his life to his Father through the Holy Spirit in reparation for our disobedience.
>
> (*CCC 614*)

Where does Watchtower teaching differ from Catholic teaching, apart from the Church's emphasis of Christ's love prompting the sacrifice, which is absent from the Watchtower definition? There are three main differences: what happened at the Fall; what Original Sin is; what was restored, and what the consequences are.

According to the Watchtower, the Fall of Adam and Eve deprived them of the perfect human life they had in Eden; 'Made with a perfect body and mind, [Adam] would never get sick, grow old, or die.... If he had chosen to obey God, he would have lived forever in Paradise.'

What Does the Bible Teach? pp. 48, 49

The Church sees things differently. It is not certain that Adam and Eve would not have died, but the death would not be the painful separation that it became after the Fall. According to the Church, there is the spiritual element in man that destined him to union with God and the Beatific Vision, and that could have been envisaged as life after death. However, we do not know what way God had planned this for us if Adam had not sinned, and neither does the Watchtower.

Original Sin

How did God create man originally? The Church says: 'God created man in his image and established him in his friendship. A spiritual creature, man can live in this friendship only in free submission to God' (*CCC 396*). This is far more than the Watchtower definition, which does not mention the spiritual element in man – as we shall see, the Watchtower denies that we have both body and a soul that survives death. The result of Adam's disobedience, original sin, 'although it is proper to each individual, original sin does not have the character of a personal fault in any of Adam's descendents [it is a state and not an act – (*CCC 404*). It is a deprivation of original holiness and justice, but human nature has not been totally corrupted: it is wounded in the natural powers proper to it, subject to ignorance, suffering and the domination of death, and inclined to sin'(*CCC 405*). We were deprived of the sanctifying grace that would enable us at that time to enter into the Beatific Vision, but not of individual grace that would enable us to respond to God's love.

This may seem somewhat academic, but it actually has profound consequences as to how we understand the effects of Christ's death on the Cross. Because, for the Watchtower, the Fall deprived us of a perfect human life lived in Paradise, then all that Jesus' death accomplished was to restore that perfect human life to be lived in a new paradise earth. Also, it needed Jesus to be only a perfect human being and not the Son of God, because only perfect human life was being restored. The Church has always seen things differently. Because the offence was committed against God, then only God could restore the friendship; since man committed the offence, then only man could make recompense. In Jesus, who is both God and man, he did what only God could do, and as a sinless man he could offer to God what man could offer.

Only a few destined for heaven

According to the Watchtower, Jesus' death on the Cross gave us all the possibility of forgiveness, but it restored to only 144,000 the opportunity of eternal life in heaven All that the Watchtower offers for the vast majority in its doctrines are the forgiveness of sins and a clean conscience before God, and the hope of everlasting life on a paradise earth and, as we shall see, not the presence of God in that paradise earth, as there was in Eden. In response, its followers are exhorted to show their appreciation by the study of the Bible and Watchtower publications, by works and by attending the annual observance of the Lord's Evening Meal. At the Lord's Meal only those who are of the 144,000 are allowed to partake of the emblems of bread and wine, and the New Covenant announced by Jesus applies only to them, who are the only ones who have the hope of going to heaven. The 'great multitude' attend 'only as respectful observers, not partakers' (*see: What the Bible Really Teaches*, pp. 53, 54, 207, 208). So according to the organisation, what was restored by Jesus' death was less than what mankind had lost through Adam's sin.

Partakers in Divine Life

The Scriptures, though, show that what was restored to us through the death and resurrection of Jesus was far more, even, than we would have had if Adam had not sinned. We are made partakers, even now, in the divine life, and what we shall be has not yet been revealed, but it will be something so great and glorious that our human minds could not conceive (*see* 1 Peter 1:3-9). We are *all* of us, all mankind, included in the New Covenant Jesus made at the Last Supper, if we accept it; the hope of heaven is offered to all. The promise is that we can begin now, while on earth, to journey into the full vision of God, and see him as he really is.(1 John 3:2) We are given a share in the glory of God, and can partake of his divine nature even here on earth. Once again, what the Watchtower offers is something far, far less than what God offers us.

PART 3

WATCHTOWER TEACHINGS

The main aim of the Jehovah's Witnesses is to convert you to their Society away from your Christian, Catholic Faith. Many Watchtower beliefs are unique to them, so these are what we will discuss next.

When a Jehovah's Witness knocks on your door, as we have seen, they home in on people's fears and apprehensions of the present, the state of the world and the country, fear for the future, fear of what is going to happen to the world. In *Reasoning From the Scriptures* the Watchtower gives its followers guidance on what to say when knocking on doors as an opening gambit, and with what to say in response to the householder's reaction. Whether it is about crime or housing, unemployment, security, the family or current events, the Witness has to focus on concerns, fears, discontent.

If they know you are a Christian, they will confront the Christian belief in heaven and hell, especially hell and how it is popularly perceived.

They also purport to give an answer to the question, What happens to us when we die? To all these issues, the answers they give are very different from the orthodox Christian response. One of the reasons for this is the different understanding between Watchtower teaching and Catholic teaching as to what the human person is, how he has been created by God, and what Catholic teaching says about his destiny. I make the distinction between Catholic and Protestant teaching on this subject, because we also differ in many ways from many Christian denominations on this.

So we must first look at what a human person is, and then explore other issues that the Jehovah's Witness might raise.

CHAPTER 11

THE IMMORTALITY OF THE SOUL

The Watchtower gives the following definition of 'soul':

> In the Bible, 'soul' is translated from the Hebrew *ne'phesh* and the Greek *psy-khe*. Bible usage shows the soul to be a person or an animal or the life that a person or an animal enjoys. To many persons, however, 'soul' means the immaterial or spirit part of a human being that survives the death of the physical body. Others understand it to be the death of life. But these latter views are not Bible teachings.
> *Reasoning From the Scriptures,* p. 375

There are two other words in Hebrew, *ruah* and *neshamah*, which, with *nephesh* have the meanings of life, breath, wind, spirit. Only *nephesh* has the additional sense of being, of a person or animal; Jesus uses it of himself in the sense of 'I' in the Garden of Gethsemane (Matthew 26:38). God himself also uses it of himself:

> Here is my servant whom I uphold,
> My chosen one in whom my soul delights
> (Isaiah 42:1)

In the Old Testament the Watchtower is correct in saying that the word 'soul' is usually translated as 'person' or 'being', meaning the whole person, body and soul; for example: 'The Lord God formed man out of the clay of the ground and blew into his nostrils the breath of life, and so man became a living being [soul] (Genesis 2:7). Likewise, '*nephesh* is used for animals: 'Then God said, "Let the earth bring forth all kinds of living creatures [souls] (Genesis 1:20).

From this, the Watchtower asserts that the Bible teaches that when a human being or an animal dies, because there is no dichotomy between soul and body, the whole being dies, ceases to exist, soul as well as body. To the Watchtower, the soul is not immortal, and cannot exist apart from the body:

> We must remember that our original father, Adam, did not *have* a soul. He *was* a soul.
>
> *Knowledge That Leads to Everlasting Life,* p. 81

In *Reasoning From the Scriptures* the Watchtower quotes from *The New Catholic Encyclopaedia* 1967, in support of its belief:

> The Christian concept of a spiritual soul created by God and infused into the body at conception to make man a living whole is the fruit of a long development in Christian philosophy. Only with Origen [died 254 C.E.] in the East and St

Augustine [died 430 C.E.] in the West was the soul established as a spiritual substance and a philosophical concept formed of its nature.... His [Augustine's] doctrine.... owed much (including some shortcomings) to Neoplatonism.' (Vol X111 pp. 452, 454).

The quotation is talking about the development of a *Christian philosophy* of the immortality of the soul. This would have been based on the Scriptural understanding on which it is based. To understand what the Scriptural basis is for the immortality of the soul, the *New Catholic Encyclopaedia* says under the entry for *Immortality*:

> That early Jewish history shows that the Hebrew nation did not believe in a future life, is sometimes stated. It is true that temporal rewards and punishments from God are much insisted upon throughout the Old Testament, and that the doctrine of a future life occupies a less prominent position there than we should perhaps have anticipated. Still, careful study of the Old Testament reveals incidental and indirect evidence quite sufficient to establish the existence of this belief among the Israelites at an early date.

Here are some texts from the Old Testament to consider:

Daniel 12:2

'Many of those who sleep in the dust of the earth shall awake; some shall live forever,

> others shall be an everlasting horror and disgrace.'

To cease to exist is not the same as falling asleep. Only a being that exists can fall asleep.

> And the dust returns to the earth as it once was, and the life breath (*ruah*) returns to the God who gave it (Ecclesiastes 12:7).

The Watchtower interpretation is 'The text does not mean that at death the spirit travels all the way to the personal presence of God; rather, any prospect for the person to live again rests with God.' (*Reasoning From the Scriptures,* p. 378). My understanding is that the text shows that the body returns to 'dust' and the spirit, that now has a separate, immortal existence, returns to God (no time travel involved!) and does not cease to exist because it is now in/with God. To say 'To live again rests with God' is a meaningless statement if, with the Watchtower, one, *a priori*, refuses to accept that God might decide that souls do *not* cease to exist.

I Kings 17:17-24 tells the story of Elijah restoring the widow's son to life. Elijah prays, (v.21) 'O Lord, my God, let the life breath (*nephesh*) return to the body of this child', and in verse 22 we are told the Lord heard the prayer of Elijah; the life breath (*nephesh*) returned to the child's body and he revived.

Therefore the soul does have a separate existence apart from the body and can be revived after the death of the body.

Interestingly, the Watchtower does believe that some elements of the human person do continue to exist - in the mind of God, as we shall see in the section on the resurrection.

So which teaching is correct, that of the Catholic Church or the Watchtower?

Gradual revelation

It is true that God did not reveal the truth of life after death fully in the Old Testament, perhaps because of the pagan beliefs that surrounded the Hebrew people, especially the elaborate beliefs of the Egyptians. There is a variety of beliefs in evidence in the Old Testament, because the people were gradually developing their thinking on the subject. To begin with, the Jews believed that they lived on in their descendents, which was one reason why the lack of an heir was such a tragedy and why they placed such an emphasis on bearing children. Gradually, however, they did come to a belief that their dead did live a shadowy existence after death. This could be seen as a waiting time between death and resurrection, sometimes with a division between the good and the wicked, who were already in hell and beyond redemption. The dead could not pray or see the light. By the time of the New Testament, the Sadducees did not believe in life after death, but the Pharisees did, as did many of the ordinary people, as we see from Martha's response to Jesus at the raising of Lazarus (John 11).

Life after death revealed by Jesus

The Old Testament came to gradual and partial recognition of the enduring quality of the soul, but it was Jesus himself who 'brought life and immortality to light through the Gospel' (2 Timothy 1:10). The Sadducees, who did not believe in life after death, came to Jesus with a trick question (Matthew 22:23-33). A woman married but her husband died, leaving her childless so, according to Jewish custom, she married his brother. This happened seven times – so whose wife was she? Jesus told them that in heaven there was no marrying or giving in marriage, taking it for granted that all were alive in heaven. He stated that since God is the God of Abraham, Isaac and Jacob, 'He is not the God of the dead but of the living.' To the Watchtower and to the Jehovah's Witnesses Jesus also says 'You are misled because you do not know the scriptures or the power of God.' Who would we rather believe, Jesus, who should know what he is talking about, or the Watchtower, which does not know the Scriptures or the power of God, since it denies the resurrection?

Other texts to ponder:

> Matt 10:28:
>
> Do not be afraid of those who can kill the body but cannot kill the soul; but rather fear him who can destroy both soul and body in hell.

Men can kill the body, but they cannot kill the soul. Only God can withdraw life from the soul. The Watchtower explanation of this text is:

> Notice that there is no mention here of *torment* in the fires of Gehenna; rather, he says to "fear him that can *destroy* in Gehenna. By referring to the "soul" separately, Jesus here emphasises that God can destroy all of a person's life prospects; thus there is no hope of resurrection for him.

By this explanation, the Watchtower is ignoring the point of Jesus' response, which is to affirm that the person, his immortal soul, does live on after death. Also, there is a difference between destruction and between annihilation of the soul, which, as we shall see, is what the Watchtower teaches.

The Watchtower objects to the doctrine of the immortality of the soul because it believes it is a pagan, especially Greek belief, adopted by the Church. However, the Church believes it because it is scriptural; it is a belief shared by billions of others who are not Christian, as it was with some of the pagan systems at the time of the Early Church. As we have seen, God prepared, not only the Jews, but also the pagans, for the truths that he would reveal in his Son so that the truths would not be totally alien to them.

Immortality of the soul

Here are more texts, among many more, to think about and how they refute the Watchtower teachings:

The Transfiguration
Mark 9
How can Moses and Elijah appear to Jesus if they no longer existed?

Philipians 1:21-24
Paul's dilemma whether to continue on earth or be with Christ. He did not believe he would cease to exist after his death.

1 Thessalonians 5:23
May the God of peace himself make you perfectly holy and may you entirely, spirit, soul and body, be preserved blameless for the coming of our Lord Jesus Christ.

Paul prays that we be preserved blameless – he certainly did not believe that at death we cease to exist.

Revelation 6:9
I saw underneath the altar the souls of those who had been slaughtered because of the witness they bore to the word of God.

Revelation 20:4
I also saw the souls of those who had been beheaded for their witness to Jesus and for the word of God.

Scientists and Surgeons?

Amazingly, the Watchtower even brings in the scientist and surgeon in support of its disbelief, regardless of the fact that the spirit, the soul, not being material, is totally outside the scope of science and surgery:

> The scientists and surgeons have come to the conclusion that man is simply a higher form of animal life, having a more complex organism and capable of exercising faculties beyond those of any of the other forms of animal life. They have not been able to find in man any definite proof of immortality. They cannot find any evidence that indicates man has an immortal soul. In contrast with this the religious leaders claim that man has an immortal soul and that this is the major difference between man and the other forms of life. They say the soul is the immortal, immaterial and spiritual part of man.
> *Let God be True,* pp. 57-58

It is very demeaning to consider that man is simply a higher form of animal life, and it is this belief that encourages the secular world to espouse abortion, euthanasia and embryo experimentation, although the Watchtower itself does not espouse these positions. In contrast, the Catholic Church sees man as created for a high destiny, of being transformed into the image of Christ and sharing forever in the very life of God. But by denying the immortality of the soul, the Watchtower does indeed deny us that higher and unique destiny.

One of the reasons why the Jehovah's Witnesses do not believe in the immortality of the soul is that Russell, the Founder of the Watchtower, did not believe in hell, so now we must examine this belief, too.

CHAPTER 12

HELL

Charles Taze Russell was a young man when he became interested in religion, and for a time was a member of the Seventh Day Adventists, who influenced many of his teachings. From their teachings on hell Russell became so disgusted with the thought of a good God inventing something as abhorrent as hell that he completely rejected it, a stance that has persisted with the Watchtower ever since.

The Organisation defines 'hell' thus:

> The word 'hell' is found in many Bible translations. In the same verses other translations read 'the grave', 'the world of the dead', and so forth. Other Bibles simply transliterate the original-language words that are sometimes rendered 'hell', that is, they express them with the letters of our alphabet but leave the words untranslated. What are these words? The Hebrew *she'ohl* and its Greek equivalent *hai'des*, which refer, not to an individual burial place, but

to the common grave of dead mankind; also the Greek *ge'en-na*, which is used as a symbol of eternal destruction. However, in both Christendom and in many non-Christian religions it is taught that hell is a place inhabited by demons and where the wicked, after death, are punished (and some believe that this is with torment).
Reasoning from the Scriptures,
pp. 168-169

Because the Watchtower does not believe in the immortality of the soul, then the Hebrew *sheol* and the Greek *hades* simply mean for the Watchtower the grave into which the body is laid. We can agree with it that when these words are rendered as 'hell' this is not a good translation, because *sheol* and *hades* do not have the idea of punishment and torment that hell usually conjures up – *gehenna* is the word for hell as a place of punishment and alienation from God.

Place of the dead

The best translation of *sheol* and *hades* is 'place of the dead', to which all went after death before the death and resurrection of Christ, except the totally wicked who had no hope of redemption. In Hebrew thought, the world consisted of heaven above, earth, and the place of the dead below the earth. It was a place of hope, because it was where the just were waiting for the redemption of Christ. They were alive in God; it was where Abraham, Isaac and Jacob resided, and as Jesus said, God is the God of the living, not the dead.

The passage from Isaiah 14:9-10 shows that the Hebrews definitely did not see *sheol* as a place of annihilation or simply the grave:

> The nether world below is all astir preparing for your coming; it awakens the shades to greet you, all the leaders of the earth. It has the kings of all the nations rise from their thrones. All of them speak out and say to you, You too have become weak like us, you are the same as we.

Reasoning from the Scriptures quotes the passage from Job 14:13, in which Job prayed 'Oh, that you would hide me in the nether world and keep me sheltered till your wrath is past; would fix a time for me, and then remember me!' The Watchtower rightly quotes this text in support of its assertion that 'hell', *sheol* is not a place of punishment, but of course the text also negates its belief that the dead are totally annihilated after death and no longer exist. Job is confident that he is still alive to God in the place of the dead. The problem is that the Watchtower equates destruction with annihilation, but something can be destroyed without being annihilated – a building, for example, can be destroyed and be reduced to a pile of rubble, which is different to being vaporised, annihilated, with nothing left.

Gehenna

Gehenna was the Jerusalem rubbish dump in the Valley of Hinnom, where the residents would throw their unwanted junk and rubbish, and where there was a continual fire and brimstone consuming whatever was thrown there; it became a fitting symbol of the destruction of the wicked which Jesus also uses. The Watchtower denies that there is eternal punishment, saying instead that it is the fire that is eternal, not the wicked cast into it.

Hell or no hell?

Since Charles Taze Russell and the Watchtower organisation after him did not believe in hell, they had to explain away these Scriptures to fit their belief. The Church has no such option. She was there in the person of St Luke when he interviewed people who had heard Jesus speaking. She had heard Jesus, say, 'Come to me, all who are heavy laden and I will give you rest'. On the other hand, she had heard him when he spoke in parables and warned that some, workers of iniquity, would find themselves thrust out from the kingdom of God, (Luke 13:28) and that others, who had not dressed themselves properly for his banquet, would not taste his feast (14:24), and that they should fear him who could cast into hell (*gehenna*) (12:14).

The Church was there when John said that God so loved the world that he gave his only-begotten Son, so that whoever believes in him should not perish but have everlasting life (3:16), and it was that John who also wrote the Book of Revelation with its horrific pictures of the battle between good and evil.

The Book of Revelation is perhaps the most misunderstood book in the Bible. Rather than being primarily a book that foretells the end of the world, John wrote it to encourage the Christians who were undergoing severe persecution, that the worship they were offering to God here on earth was a reflection of the heavenly liturgy, that their sufferings would result in their triumph over death, and that evil and death would not have the final word. He uses the apocalyptic language of the time to convey this. Only in a secondary sense does it look forward to the Final Judgement.

Because the Church has been given the authority to preach the Good News she has to preach the whole of it. It was Jesus himself who said that some would rise to eternal life and others to eternal punishment. (John 5:29. cf. Daniel 2:12). But why does punishment for sin and separation from God have to be eternal?

Eternal punishment

God made us with immortal, imperishable, souls, infused into the embryo at conception, because he destines every single one of us to be with him for all eternity. If we freely refuse that gift, he cannot change who we are as human beings, that is, beings created for an *eternal* destiny. We are created for eternal life, but God does not force it on to us; he offers us eternal life, he invites us to share his life for all eternity. However, we can accept or refuse that offer, that gift; we can refuse his love and we can refuse to live the sort of life that will fit us to be immersed in the love of God (this is the meaning of the parable of the man who has no wedding garment of Luke 14). Perhaps the key to the Book of Revelation lies in verse 3:20 – 'Behold, I stand at the door and knock. If anyone hears my voice and opens the door, [then] I will enter his house and dine with him, and he with me.'

The famous picture of Holman Hunt, '*the Light of the World*', depicting this scene shows the door with the key on the inside. Jesus stands outside our door knocking. We have the power to turn the key and allow Jesus in, or we can keep him shut out of our lives. This second option is hell, that is, life without accepting the love and life of God. Because to have an immortal soul is what it means to be a person, then if we choose that second option, then that is what we choose for all eternity.

What God wills

God's will is for all men to be saved and come to the knowledge of the truth, and his infinite love has provided everything it possibly could to make that happen. But he has also given us free will, because he will not force us to love him. He wants our love to be freely given. Therefore, there has to be the possibility that we will refuse to give him that love; therefore the Church has to believe in hell, which is the rejection of the love of God for the option of being with ourselves, without God, for all eternity. However, the Church has not said that anyone is actually in that state, and never could, because only God can know that.

The Watchtower, however, does know! One Jehovah's Witness was adamant that Adam and Eve were not redeemed, that they were beyond the reach of the Ransom Sacrifice of Jesus. Also, according to the Watchtower, all the righteous men who lived before Christ's sacrifice on the Cross, cannot be numbered among the 144,000. And of course they condemn all non-Jehovah Witnesses as being beyond the Ransom Sacrifice of God.

God a vindictive torturer?

The idea of eternal punishment does not make God into a vindictive torturer, although this is a common misapprehension. He is a Judge, not an executioner. Hell is a state which the wicked have willingly and with full knowledge chosen for themselves, and the punishment of eternal separation from God that they must endure is only what is due to their sins and their choice. They are their own 'executioners'. Furthermore, no suffering that could possibly be inflicted on them would equal that which is the very essence of hell itself - to endure for all eternity the realization that they have closed upon themselves, by their own free choice, and with full understanding, the gateway to salvation, that they have denied to themselves what their souls were designed and predestined for, to be united with God and live his life of love for all eternity. Instead, they have chosen self apart from the God who created them and for whom they were created. This is the denial of that hope which is at the heart of the New Testament message of salvation.

Catholic teaching

The Catholic Church teaches that:

> 'We cannot be united with God unless we freely choose to love him' (*CCC 1033*).

> The teaching of the Church affirms the existence of hell and its eternity. Immediately after death the souls of those who die in a state of mortal sin descend into hell, where they suffer the punishment of "eternal fire". The chief punishment of hell is eternal separation from God, in whom alone man can possess the life and happiness for which he was created and for which he longs (*CCC 1035*).

> God predestines no one to go to hell; for this, a wilful turning away from God (a mortal sin) is necessary, and a persistence in it until the end (*CCC 1037*).

Seeing God after death?

One problem of accepting the idea of hell is that atheists and non-believers may have such a distorted understanding of God that it may well be that they are rejecting a totally false understanding of who God really is. Richard Dawkins famously described God as

> arguably the most unpleasant character in all fiction: jealous and proud of it; a petty, unjust, unforgiving control-freak; a vindictive, bloodthirsty, ethnic cleanser; a misogynistic, homophobic, racist, infanticidal, genocidal, filicidal, pestilential, megalomaniacal, sado-masochistic, capriciously malevolent bully.

If this is honestly how Dawkins sees God, then it is no wonder that he should reject him, and so should we, if he really is that sort of god. Therefore, it is possible that at death each one of us will see God as he really is, not as our limited human and perhaps distorted understanding of him is. It is the True God whom we must accept or reject.

Purgatory

As with non-Catholic denominations, the Watchtower rejects the idea of Purgatory as unscriptural, and of course, since it does not believe in heaven or hell, then it has to reject purgatory. Although the word itself does not appear in Scripture the implication of a purgatorial, purifying state certainly is. Jesus himself says that there are some sins against the Holy Spirit that cannot be forgiven *either on earth or heaven* (Matthew 12:32, emphasis mine), implying that there are sins that can be forgiven in heaven, that is, after death. The Book of Maccabees in the Old Testament (2 Maccabees 12) speaks of praying for the dead. Protestants do not accept the books of Maccabees as part of the inspired canon of the Old Testament, but since the Catholic Church had accepted what are called the apocryphal books from the time of the Apostles, because they formed part of the Septuagint, the Greek translation of the Old Testament used by the Apostles and from the earliest Church onwards, we Catholics can accept their testimony.

An important text, though, is 1 Corinthians 3:10-15. In this text, Paul says (vv. 12-15):

> if anyone builds on this foundation with gold, silver, precious stones, wood, hay or straw, the work of each will come to light, for the Day will disclose it. It will be revealed with fire, and the fire [itself] will test the quality of each one's work. If the work stands that someone built upon the foundation, that person will receive a wage. But if someone's work is burned up, that one will suffer loss; the person will be saved, but only as through fire.

This passage coincides with the Catholic understanding of purgatory. The person is saved because he has built on the foundation of Christ. He is standing before Christ after his death, on the day of his judgment. His works are of varying value; the good works of the imperishable materials of holiness, of gold, silver, precious stones, will withstand the fire, but the perishable ones of wood, hay, straw, will be burnt up; therefore it involves purification.

One vital thing to bear in mind is that purgatory is part of heaven; those in purgatory are assured of their eternal salvation in heaven, and so there is a tremendous hope and assurance that the intense desire to be fully united with God and enjoy the eternal vision of him, will be fulfilled, once the dust of their earthly journey has been consumed away through the action of the love of God within their souls. Our one desire in purgatory is to be totally fit and pure to share that vision, because nothing impure can enter heaven (Revelation 21:27). As the *Catechism of the Catholic Church* explains (1030): 'All who die in God's grace and friendship, but still imperfectly purified, are indeed assured of their eternal salvation; but after death they undergo purification, so as to achieve the holiness necessary to enter the joy of heaven.' It is the burning love of God which purifies us.

CHAPTER 13

THE RESURRECTION

The Resurrection of Jesus

On the third day of his being dead in the grave his immortal Father Jehovah God raised him [Jesus] from the dead, not as a human Son, but as a mighty immortal spirit Son, with all power in heaven and earth under the Most High God. Says the Jewish witness, Peter: 'Being put to death in the flesh, but made alive in the spirit.' (1 Peter 3:18). For forty days thereafter he materialized, as angels before him had done, to show himself alive to his disciples as witnesses. He then ascended to heaven and appeared in God's presence with the value of his human sacrifice as God's High Priest, and this he applied in behalf of all those who should believe in him (Hebrews 9:11, 23, 24; 10:12,13).

Let God Be True, p. 43

This is the Watchtower version of the Resurrection of Christ, and of course it differs from the Christian understanding. The quotation from 1 Peter is one that the Watchtower uses frequently to oppose the Christian belief that Jesus rose in a risen body, which is different, as Jesus himself said, from being a spirit. Jesus specifically said:

> While they were still speaking about this, he stood in their midst and said to them, 'Peace be with you'. But they were startled and terrified and thought they were seeing a ghost. Then he said to them, 'Why are you troubled? And why do questions arise in your hearts? Look at my hands and my feet, that it is I myself. Touch me and see, because a ghost does not have flesh and bones as you see I have' (Luke 24:36-39).

Jesus then showed them his hands and his feet, with the marks of the nails visible, and then ate a piece of baked fish to show them that he was no ghost, spirit or apparition. Note that the text says that *he*, Jesus, was made alive in the spirit, and the Watchtower always affirms that the person is both body and soul, indivisible, so therefore when it says that Jesus was made alive in the spirit, it must surely be, according to Watchtower's own teaching, that it refers to the whole Jesus, body and soul, with his body sharing in the resurrection.

On *Reasoning From the Scriptures* (p. 334) the Watchtower gives its own explanation of this passage, saying that 'he was a spirit creature and when, as angels had done in the past, he materialized fleshly bodies to make himself visible.'

When a Jehovah's Witness gave me this explanation, I was literally speechless; not primarily because of the explanation or my ability to respond, but because she could so blithely contradict Jesus himself, when he said he was not a spirit, as to say, 'Oh yes, he was!' It hurt me deeply that, indoctrinated by the Watchtower, she had so little respect and regard for Jesus and what he said.

It was pointless to argue the issue at this juncture, because the Witnesses believe Jesus was an angel, which made the explanation perfectly acceptable to them, but is profoundly wrong to a Catholic.

The Watchtower accepts that Jesus' body was no longer in the tomb and has God somehow materialising it away; but in his post-resurrection appearances Jesus was at pains to show that there was a fundamental relationship between his existence before his Crucifixion and his Risen life afterwards, and that involved his body. This is what St Paul tells us in the comparison with the seed and the full wheat: 'What you sow is not the body which is to be but a bare kernel of wheat, perhaps, or of some other kind; but God gives it a body as he chooses. It is sown corruptible; it is raised incorruptible' (1 Corinthians 15:37, 42). There is a natural and intrinsic connection between the two, just as there is a natural connection between the grain of wheat that is sown in the ground and springs up as an ear of wheat, not the total disconnection the Watchtower asserts.

There is also the text from Romans 8:10-11, which states:

> If the Spirit of the one who raised Jesus from the dead dwells in you, the one who raised Christ from the dead will give life to your mortal bodies, also, through his Spirit that dwells in you.

This makes it perfectly clear that Paul – and the Church – had no concept of the thoughts, ideas, memories etc, of either Jesus or ourselves being stored in God's memory, to be reconstituted in a newly fashioned body at some time or other. What was being raised, in Jesus' case, was the whole person to a totally new, resurrected life – the Watchtower itself says that the person is indivisible – and in our case we, too, will be raised with our physical bodies that will share in the transformation into a risen body, as Jesus' was, at the Last Judgment.

By denying the reality of the bodily resurrection of Jesus, the Watchtower is also denying our bodily resurrection, too.

As a personal reflection: because it is the spirit, the soul, that endures beyond death, then is it not feasible that, prior to the resurrection of the body at the Last Judgment, there will be some form of the body that also survives? We can see in the examples of some of the saints that even their bodies shared in the transformation of their souls in Christ even while they lived, that their bodies already had some of the glory that would be theirs in heaven.

Our resurrection

Since the Watchtower teaches that we are totally annihilated and cease to exist at death, it had to explain how, at a future date, we nevertheless come back to life to go either to heaven or to paradise earth. It had to come up with an alternative to the immortal soul. Since, to the organisation, Jesus, too, was a human being, at his death the same pertained to his condition after death. The Watchtower therefore defines Resurrection as involving

> a reactivating of the life pattern of the individual, which life pattern God has retained in his memory. According to God's will for the individual, the person

is restored in either a human or a spirit body and yet retains his personal identity, having the same personality and memories as when he died.
Reasoning from the Scriptures, p. 333

What if the true God decides to restore the 'spirit' of life to that person? With His perfect memory, God can remember exactly what the person was like. It is similar to what men today do when they use magnetic tapes to record the voices and actions of people and reproduce these by radio or on a video screen long after these persons have died. Truly it will not be difficult for God, the Creator, with His infinite memory, to remake a human from the dust of the earth, incorporate in him every detail of his previous personality and mind, and restore his spirit, or life-force, so that he lives again.
Good News –to Make You Happy, pp. 93, 94

When they come back will they be the same person? Will we know them? Yes! Even man can indefinitely preserve pictures and voices on magnetic tape for later use on television. God can do even more than that. At resurrection time he can provide each one with a suitable body, just as he did in creating the first man, and then reimplant in the brain the exact memories of all that the person learned and experienced during his former life. Thus in the resurrection that person will come forth with the same personality that he had at death, just as the resurrected Jesus retained his own personality (Hebrews 13:8).

*The Truth That Leads to
Eternal Life,* pp. 109, 111

Understandably, the Watchtower gives no Scripture reference for this idea, as this supposition has no foundation in Scripture. The quotation from Hebrews 13: 8 'Christ is the same yesterday is the same yesterday, today and forever' in this context is not referring to his Resurrection. The problem with this definition is that a person's life pattern, his memories and experience are not the sum of that person, and to remake a life pattern would not be resurrecting the same human person, who in any case has been annihilated, but infusing a different, 'suitable' body with the annihilated person's life pattern, memories and experience. A newborn baby, who has no memories or experience outside the womb, is still a human person.

As so often with the quotations the Watchtower uses, in citing Hebrews 13:8 'this does not 'prove'' the Watchtower interpretation. In fact, according to its teaching, Jesus is *not* the same yesterday, today and forever, for it teaches that Jesus was first of all a spirit creature, Michael the Archangel, then he became a man, no longer an angel, then reverted back to being Michael the Archangel – therefore no continuity.

The Resurrection of Jesus

Since Jesus, according to the Watchtower, is simply a human being, then he, too, was totally annihilated when he died on the cross. How, then, was he resurrected? According to the Watchtower, he is resurrected (or rather, reconstituted) in the same way as everyone else, from the elements stored in God's memory. The body in which he appeared after his resurrection was simply a manufactured body for that particular appearance, with no reference to the body that was no longer in the tomb.

> Humans cannot see spirits, so the disciples evidently thought they were seeing an apparition or a vision (cf. Mark 6:49, 50). Jesus assured them that he was no apparition; they could see his body of flesh and could touch him, feeling the bones; he also ate in their presence. Similarly, in the past, angels had materialized in order to be seen by men; they had eaten, and some had even married and fathered children (Genesis 6:4; 19:1-3). Following his resurrection, Jesus did not always appear in the same body of flesh (perhaps to reinforce in their minds the fact that he was then a spirit), and so he was not immediately recognised even by his close associates (John 20:14, 15; 21:4-7). However, by his repeatedly appearing to them in materialized bodies and then saying and doing things that they would identify with the Jesus they knew, he strengthened their faith in the fact that he had been resurrected from the dead.
>
> *Reasoning From the Scriptures,*
> pp. 334-335

As we have already seen, the Watchtower equates Jesus' appearances with those of angels, but Jesus' resurrected being was not of the angelic order, but a completely different mode of being. The reference to Genesis 6:4 is misleading, because it does not refer to angels. Even the Watchtower NWT does not specify the beings as angels. The Nephilim probably were simply very tall men and thus were thought to be of semi-divine origin.

Some biblical scholars have also used the references the Watchtower gives of people not immediately recognising Jesus to question the reality of the bodily resurrection of Jesus. However, even in the natural course of events there is a rational explanation. Mary was not expecting Jesus to be alive, so it was understandable that, with her eyes full of tears she did not recognise him until he spoke to her. The disciples in the boat were some way from shore. Luke specifically said of the disciples on the way to Emmaus Luke 24: 13-35) 'their eyes were kept from recognising him'.

Mary recognised Jesus when she heard his voice speaking her name; the disciples in the boat recognised Jesus with the recognition of the heart. It was not a question of Jesus having a different body each time he appeared. It was truly he, in his risen and glorified body, although that glory was hidden, who appeared to the disciples. When he showed the disciples the wounds in his body, those wounds were on the same body that had been crucified and now reigns triumphantly in heaven (Rev 5:6 note d) in the Jerusalem Bible says:

- The Messiah, the Passover lamb sacrificed for the Salvation of the Chosen People. The wounds that caused the death of the Lamb are visible, but the Lamb has risen from death, and therefore stands upright. The Messiah, who became a lamb in order to submit as sacrifice, to suffer and to die, is a lion because he conquered death.

The Gospel writers also have a message for us in these Resurrection appearances. Like Mary, we recognise Jesus when he speaks our name, when our hearts burn within us as he speaks his word to us, when he meets us in our daily lives, when we meet him, above all, in the Eucharist, the 'breaking of bread'.

The Raising of Lazarus

Another time one of my sessions with the Jehovah's Witnesses began with a discussion about the raising of Lazarus. As we have seen, the Watchtower teaches that after death there is nothing. We 'fall asleep' and are conscious of nothing because we no longer exist, until, if we are Jehovah's Witnesses, we are resurrected (reconstituted), to paradise earth. In support of this belief, 'how could Lazarus have possibly survived coming back to earth after the bliss of being in the presence of God', asked the Witness? If, however, he was conscious of nothing at all after death, she said, then there would be no problem.

Of course, since Jesus had not yet died and risen, Lazarus would not have been in heaven but in the patient peacefulness of *sheol* with the other patriarchs and just men awaiting Jesus' descent into *sheol* after his death, to bring out those that were in prison (1 Peter 3:18). It could be, though, that God did not allow him to have any memory of his time in the tomb, although there are countless accounts of people who have had Near Death Experiences and have returned to tell of them. We do not know.

Resurrection or resuscitation?

The Watchtower sees no difference between the Resurrection of Jesus, where Jesus is raised to a new form of existence, where he can die no more and lives for ever, and the instances of resuscitation from death, such as Lazarus and the widow's son, where they are brought back temporarily to earthly life, but would die again.

The Watchtower does not see any difference between these instances of raising to life that Jesus performed, even though I pointed out that those who were raised to life would die again, whereas Jesus, having died once, will never die again. Neither could the widow's son and Lazarus subsequently come through locked doors. Jesus' Resurrection belongs to a totally different sphere of reality.

Brought to life in the spirit

The Watchtower does not believe that the body can go to heaven, quoting 1 Corinthians 15:50: 'This I declare, brothers, flesh and blood cannot inherit the kingdom of heaven, nor does corruption inherit corruption'. In *Reasoning From the Scriptures* p. 334, the Watchtower prefaces this verse with a quotation from 1 Peter 3:18: 'Put to death in the flesh, he was brought to life in the spirit.' It interprets this as saying that Jesus, at his resurrection, was brought forth with a 'spirit body' and also as contrasting flesh and spirit.

It is true that Saint Paul, especially, often contrasts flesh and spirit: 'those who are in the flesh cannot please God,' he writes to the Romans (8:8), but he goes on to say, 'But you are not in the flesh; on the contrary, you are in the spirit, if the Spirit of God dwells in you' (v 9). St Paul often uses 'flesh' to describe the disordered, earthly way of living, not as describing our bodies. It is precisely because we have been born again by water and the Spirit in baptism that even our mortal bodies will put on immortality. 'If the Spirit of him who raised Jesus Christ from the dead is living in you, then he who raised Jesus from the dead will give life to your own mortal bodies through his Spirit living in you. (v. 11) Romans 8:1-13 needs to be read in its entirety to see what Paul's argument is, which is what the Catholic Church teaches. When Paul says that Jesus was raised in the spirit, he means that it was the Holy Spirit working within his mortal body that raised him to resurrected life.

Comfort of oblivion after death

I attended the funeral of a family friend who, although not a Jehovah's Witness, was sympathetic to them and received a Witness funeral. The Kingdom Servant gave a talk in which he drew almost totally on Old Testament texts to explain that there was no hell to fear after death, because our friend would be in the oblivion of sleep – he did not mention that our friend would be totally annihilated. He explained it as a comfort that there was no fear of hell, only the prospect of a future paradise earth. This is what another Witness found comforting:

> I think the impartial reader will concede to the Witnesses in all fairness that the future hope of life after death which they offer to their faithful followers is a more comforting one than the orthodox for two reasons. First, the hope of eternal life in a Paradise earth is more easily imaginable than that of the eternal bliss in heaven, of which none of us can have any real conception at all. And second, although

> it is true that the Witnesses teach that death means complete non-existence, this does not really detract from the comfort offered by their re-creation hope. For in viewing death as a sleep, they rightly point out that in sleep there is no awareness of the passage of time. One could sleep for a thousand years and not know it, as in the famous fairy-tale of Rip Van Winkle. So if a Witness dies today, he is comforted in this thought, that it will just be like going to sleep today, and waking up tomorrow morning in Paradise. I can think of no better teaching for taking the sting out of death.[20]

This passage offers, as the writer suggests, some comfort, the comfort offered to the people at my friend's funeral, that all they need look forward to is a sleep, not the thought of heaven or the horrible prospect of hell. Firstly, it misunderstands the Christian understanding of heaven. After death, time no longer exists. We will be in the eternity of God, so the comparison of waking up after a long sleep no longer applies. I agree when Stevenson says that the Witness's Paradise earth is more easily imaginable – after all, it is the work of the human imagination. Jesus never describes what heaven will be like, because, as Saint Paul says, it is beyond human imagination. 'No eye has seen, no ear has heard, neither has it entered into the heart of man, what God has prepared for those who love him' (1 Corinthians 2:9). We do know that 'what we are to be in the future has not yet been revealed; all we know is, that

---

[20] W. C. Stevenson, *The Inside Story of the Jehovah's Witnesses* (New York City, Hart Publishing Company, 1967), p. 126.

when it is revealed we shall be like him because we shall see him as he really is.' (1 John 3:2). Surely this is the far more wonderful hope that the Scriptures open up to us. What God has in store for us is far beyond anything that our limited human imagination can conjure up. Why should we reject something so wonderful because it is beyond our human imagining?

However, living to the full a Christian life here on earth does give us some apprehension of what the fullness will be after our death. So many saints cry out, 'I want to see God!' St Peter says:

> You did not see him, yet you love him; and still without seeing him, you are already filled with joy so glorious that it cannot be described, because you believe; and you are sure of the end to which your faith looks forward, that is, the salvation of your souls.
>
> 1 Peter 1:8, 9

This is what God wills for us, and for which we were created. I do not want a paradise earth where Jesus is not. What is so painful is that the Watchtower seeks to deprive its followers of this glorious destiny, although, of course, it is not in its gift to do so.

A new creation

The Catholic understanding is that in his new and transformed existence after the Resurrection, we are freed from the limitations and weaknesses of human life. It is true that 'flesh and blood' human beings in their natural state of limitations, sins and weaknesses cannot inherit the kingdom of heaven, but 1 Corinthians 15 also makes the point that the Resurrection of Jesus has transformed, not only his own body into a glorious body that will never see corruption, but has also given power to human beings also to be transformed from glory to glory and to share his own glory and inherit the kingdom of heaven. When does this begin to happen? In baptism, when we went down into the waters in sacramental death with Jesus and rose to the new life of his resurrection, even in this life. (Romans 6:4) This is a foretaste of the final resurrection when we shall be united, body and soul.

This is totally alien to Watchtower beliefs, so we now have to consider what it does offer its followers.

CHAPTER 14

THE 144,000

The Watchtower teaches that there are two futures, two hopes, awaiting faithful Jehovah's Witnesses: one group, the 'little flock' of 144,000, will be raised (or reconstituted) with spirit bodies, the rest, the great crowd with physical bodies, to enjoy a paradise on earth. The 144,000 will govern earth from heaven. This limiting of the fullness of Christ's redemption to only 144,000 is one of the most disturbing teachings of the Watchtower organization.

Little Flock?

When Jesus spoke of the 'little flock' in Luke 12:32, the verse says that he was speaking to his disciples at this point rather than to the crowds of people in verse 1. There is no indication that Jesus was limiting his promise of the kingdom to his twelve disciples (including Judas at that time!), and no warrant whatsoever for the Watchtower to link it to the 144,000 of Revelation 7:4. The Church, of course, applies this text to all disciples of Jesus, for the Gospel is written for all.

According to the Watchtower,
- Only the 144,000 are born again of water and the spirit (John 3:5).

  Reasoning from the Scriptures, p. 76
- Only the 144,000 are with Christ (or the Michael the Archangel!) in his heavenly kingdom. They share in the government that Jesus exercises from heaven. However, Jesus will not rule over those who will live in the paradise earth, but over only the 144,000 in heaven. So those of the 'great multitude will have no contact with Jesus, their true Saviour, but only with the Watchtower, which has become their new 'saviour'.
- People can have faith in Christ and yet not be part of this select band. The Watchtower quotes John 1:12, 13 – 'To those who did accept him he gave power to become children of God, to those who believe in his name, who were born not by natural generation nor by human choice nor by man's decision but of God.' The Watchtower explanation of this text is:

> 'as many as did receive him' [NWT] does not mean all humans who have put faith in Christ. Notice who is being referred to, as indicated by verse 11 ['his own people' the Jews]. The same privilege has been extended to others of mankind, but only to a 'little flock.']
>
> *Reasoning From the Scriptures,* p. 77

So the Watchtower saw that if it interpreted this text literally it would apply only to the Jews, therefore it immediately discards this literal application and applies it to the 'little flock' as well, but only to them, without any justification whatsover. Rather, 'those who accept him' does not apply only to the Jews of the previous verse, as the Watchtower states, but also 'to those who believe in his name'. God's gift of becoming his children is extended to all. Jew and Gentile alike.

The Watchtower then applies 1 Peter 1:3, 4 *only* to the 'little flock':

> Blessed be the God and Father of our Lord Jesus Christ, who in his great mercy gave us a new birth to a living hope through the resurrection of Jesus Christ from the dead. To an inheritance that is imperishable, undefiled and unfading, kept in heaven for you.

Ordinary Jehovah's Witnesses, or the 'Jonadabs' (see Joshua 10:10-27), as the Watchtower sometimes calls them, can never be born anew to the living hope, and it goes without saying that no-one who is not a Jehovah's Witness can have that living hope, either.

This is another example where the Watchtower applies a Scripture promise to a limited number of people. The Catholic Church, when fixing the canon of the New Testament, gave the Scriptures to all. 'To *all* those who accept him' is the promise given. Human authorities such as Russell, Rutherford, Knorr and their descendants, and the Watchtower, cannot snatch your inheritance and hope away from you!

One fold

One Jehovah's Witness quoted to me John 10:16 – I have other sheep who do not belong to this fold' to support the Watchtower doctrine of two 'folds' one for the 144,000, and one for the 'great multitude'. However, as so often, the Witnesses are very selective in their quotations. I continued the full quotation of the verse that the Witness had omitted, because Our Lord goes on directly to say – in the very same verse! - 'These also I must lead, and they will hear my voice, and there will be *one flock*, one shepherd.' (emphasis mine). Jesus here was referring to the Gentiles who would become one flock with the Jewish people who believed in him. St Paul also reiterates that there is 'one body, one Spirit, as you were also called to the one hope of your call: one Lord, one faith, one baptism, one God and Father of all' (Ephesians 4:4-6). It is totally unscriptural for the Watchtower to divide their followers into two classes, with two hopes.

What about the 144,000?

This number appears in Revelation 7: 1-8 and Revelation 14: 1-4. It is interesting that in my early encounters with the Jehovah's Witnesses, they referred only to Revelation 7, without mentioning Revelation 14. In a visit a few years later they referred only to Revelation 14. When I tried to draw their attention to the earlier text they refused to do so – perhaps because by then it had been pointed out to them often enough in their door to door visits that in that text the 144,000 were those still on the earth (because the angels were standing at the four corners of the earth) and from the twelve tribes of Israel, and it was the 'great multitude' who were standing before the throne and before the Lamb – that is, in heaven, not in a 'paradise earth'. The Scripture says exactly the opposite to what the Watchtower was saying!

Its interpretation of the verse is that 'standing before the throne and before the Lamb' indicates, not necessarily a location, but an approved condition' (*Reasoning From the Scriptures,* p. 167). In one sense that is correct, because there is no time and space in heaven, but John was using figurative language to express the inexpressible. His obvious intention was to say that in heaven we will be in the presence of God. It is true that we *are* in relationship with the throne of God and of the Lamb – for Jesus said that we will be where he is, (cf John 17:24), although what an 'approved condition' is, I don't know!

Who, then, are the 144,000, (12,000 x 12)? The text can be interpreted in two ways – that the 144,000 are the fullness of the Jewish nation, or that it refers to the new Israel of all the redeemed. If it refers to the Jewish people, then this is supported by other texts. In Revelation 14:1, 3 they sing a song that no others can sing because of their special relationship with God as the Chosen People. Compare also Romans 11 especially verse 26 – all Israel will be saved.

The Watchtower does not in fact limit membership of the 144,000 only to Jews, as it would have to do if it wished to be consistent with its interpretation of this verse, but also to select Jehovah's Witnesses. It explains the inconsistency by saying that the tribes listed are not the original twelve tribes of Israel. No, they are not, but the tribes were reorganised as time went on. It does not detract from the fact that the members of the tribes were Jewish - verse 29 – and the gifts and the call of God are irrevocable. God never has and never will withdraw his promises, his Covenant, from his chosen people, the Jews, even though Christians now have the New Covenant, renewed at every Mass in the offering and the sharing in of Christ's Body and Blood.

Memorial meal

The Witnesses celebrate what they call the Memorial Meal just once a year around the Feast of the Passover, because the Watchtower says that the Eucharist is different from the Last Supper, and so it is only the Last Supper they commemorate. As with most Protestant denominations the Watchtower understands the word memorial or remembrance in the secular sense of the word as a commemoration of a dead person or an event that remains in the past. This is not remembrance in the Scriptural understanding of that word, *zachar,* which is a making present of a past event, and of course, in the Mass we are making present an ever-living Person. We are not remembering a dead person! Again, like Protestant denominations, the Watchtower does not see the bread and wine as transformed into the body, blood, soul and divinity of Jesus Christ, as his words affirm - 'This *is* My Body, this *is* My Blood (emphases added). The Watchtower renders those words to fit into its own belief, 'This means my body'. In John 6 Jesus was so emphatic that he really meant that we should eat his body and drink his blood, refusing to water down his words, that some of his disciples walked away, not able to take it. At the Last Supper Jesus revealed how this was to happen. Catholics and Orthodox, even though we can never fully fathom this tremendous gift, say with St Peter, 'Master, to whom shall we go? You have the words of eternal life' (John 6:68).

With many Protestant denominations the Watchtower makes what seems to be a valid objection that at the last Supper Jesus meant the bread and the wine to be only symbolic, because how he could he give his disciples his body and blood to eat and drink when he was present there with them?

However, it is important to read the actual words of consecration the Lord spoke, and which are repeated at every Mass:

> Take this, all of you, and eat of it, for this is my Body, which will be given up for you. Take this, all of you, and drink from it, for this is the chalice of my Blood, the Blood of the new and eternal Covenant, which will be poured out for you and for many for the forgiveness of sins.

The Body and Blood that the Lord is giving his disciples is the Body and Blood that *will be* offered up on the Cross. Jesus is giving the new People of God a New Covenant, and as in the Old Testament, a covenant has to be ratified by blood and a partaking in the victim offered up. At the Last Supper, Jesus is transcending time. The offering up of the sacrificial victim is already taking place.

That is why the Church carefully preserves Jesus' exact words at the Consecration of the Mass. The priest does not say 'that was given up, or 'was poured out', because the Mass is not a memorial meal recalling a past event. The priest is making present what Catholics call 'the Paschal Mystery', the whole movement of the Covenant ratified on the Cross and consummated at the Resurrection.

Watchtower Memorial Meal

Only those who consider themselves one of the 144,000 partake of the bread and wine at the Memorial Meal, with the other Witnesses only 'exercising faith'.

> 'Eleven faithful followers to whom Jesus said "I make a covenant with you, just as my Father has made a covenant with me, for a kingdom.' (Luke 22:29, NWT). They were all persons who were being invited to share with Christ in his heavenly kingdom.

> All who partake of the bread and wine today should also be persons whom Christ brings into that 'covenant for a kingdom'.
> *Reasoning from the Scriptures,*
> pp. 267, 268

In other words, the New Covenant Jesus inaugurated at the Last Supper applies, in Watchtower teaching, to only 144,000, because only they 'would receive the heavenly Kingdom as their reward' (*ibid.,* p. 268). If it was being logical, of course, it would need to limit the Covenant to only the eleven disciples!

This section adds that 'Reasonably, there would be only a small number partaking now'. Interestingly, in statistics released by the Watchtower for the year 1948 some 25,000 members partook of the memorial meal, with a steady dip in the years following, until 2007 when the number was 9105, since when the number has started increasing to 10857 in 2009. Previously, it had been stated that the number had been reached by 1935, (*The Watchtower, 15/2/1995*). It made accommodation for more to be added because some of the 144,000 had failed to adhere to Watchtower teachings and become 'evil servants'. None of the Watchtower literature says how a Witness decides if he or she is one of the 144,000, (who are now called the Remnant), or not.

At the Memorial Meal the elements are passed round to the non-partaking. If none of those present consider themselves as part of the 144,000, then no-one partakes of them.

Since only the 144,000 will be in heaven, what will that heaven be like for these favoured few, and what will they do there?

CHAPTER 15

HEAVEN

The Watchtower defines heaven as:

> The dwelling place of Jehovah God and of faithful spirit creatures; a realm invisible to human eyes. The Bible also uses the term 'heaven(s) in a variety of other senses; for example: to represent God himself, his organization of faithful spirit creatures, a position of divine favour, the physical universe apart from the earth, the expanse surrounding planet Earth, human governments under Satan's domination, and the righteous new heavenly government in which Jesus Christ with his joint heirs are empowered by Jehovah to rule.
> *Reasoning from the Scriptures,* p. 161

With such a meagre and emasculated definition of heaven, it is understandable that the Watchtower can easily persuade its followers that a paradise earth has much more to recommend it. It goes to great lengths to persuade their followers that the vast majority of them will not go to heaven, however good, faithful, pure and holy they might be. Further, the Watchtower takes to itself the authority to state who will or who will not, go to heaven.

Those who are not Jehovah's Witnesses will not go to heaven, neither will those born before the birth of Christ. Neither will those Jehovah's Witnesses who have shown 'bad attitude' and not been fervent in proseletyising and in Watchtower service.

Only 144,000 of Jehovah's Witnesses will be in heaven as spirit creatures to be ruled by Christ. This, according to the Watchtower, seems to be the only reason to be in heaven. The only question it asks about these 144,000 is 'What will they do in heaven?' The answer is that since they will rule as kings with him [Christ] for a thousand years, they must have subjects to rule over, that is, the great multitude on paradise earth.

The Watchtower does not describe itself as a church but as an incorporated organisation – the Watchtower Bible and Tract Society of New York, Inc., so it is not surprising that it sees heaven as a government. There is no hint in any of its books and tracts that I have read that they see in heaven there is love of God, worship of him, praise, joy or adoration.

What does the Catholic Faith say of heaven?

Heaven

Those who die in God's grace and friendship and are perfectly purified to live for ever with Christ. They are like God for ever, for they 'see him as he is' face to face' (1 John 3:2) (CCC 1023).

This perfect life with the Most Holy Trinity – this communion of life and love with the Trinity, with the Virgin Mary, the angels and all the blessed – is called 'heaven'. Heaven is the ultimate end and fulfilment of the deepest human longings, the state of supreme, definitive happiness (CCC 1024).

To be in heaven is 'to be with Christ' (CCC 1025).

This mystery of blessed communion with God and all who are in Christ is beyond all understanding and description. Scripture speaks of it in images: life, light, peace, wedding feast, wine of the kingdom, the Father's house, the heavenly Jerusalem, paradise; 'no eye has seen, nor ear heard, nor has the heart of man conceived, what God has prepared for those who love him' (1 Corinthians 2:9) (CCC1027).

The whole of this section of the Catechism of the Catholic Church 1023 – 1032 deserves to be meditated on and to compare it with the Watchtower 'heaven', to see what a poor and meagre understanding the Watchtower has of the wonderful reality God offers to all and which we can, even now, catch a glimpse.

Reigning as kings

The Watchtower is correct in that the Scriptures do see the redeemed in Heaven reigning as kings, but it can only see that as ruling over other people. How does the Church see us as reigning as kings?

By our baptism, every Christian is priest, prophet and king, sharing in Jesus' royal priesthood. We share in the 'blood royal' when we partake of his Precious Blood in the Eucharist. But Jesus said that his Kingdom was not of this world, and therefore his and our kingship is different from earthly kingship. Jesus is the Servant King, and he reigned from the Cross. He is the humble King, and so his followers must be like him. Christians share in the kingship of Christ when they have overcome themselves through the grace of God, they have become victorious over sin and death. It is not a question of ruling over others. We will reign as kings because we have overcome ourselves, our sins and weaknesses through the action of the grace of God.

If only the 144,000 will inherit heaven, then the rest of the Jehovah's Witnesses, the Jonadabs have a paradise earth to look forward to. First of all though, they look forward to the joyful event of Armageddon. We have to find out when the Watchtower says this event will take place, and then what it involves.

CHAPTER 16

1914 AND ALL THAT

Charles Taze Russell was influenced by the milleniarist ideas floating around in the late nineteenth century, and especially by the Seventh Day Adventists. Despite the fact that Jesus warned his followers not to speculate on when the end of the world would occur, (Matthew 24:36), the Watchtower and other sects have done so ever since, and none more so than many American 'milleniarist' sects. Russell soon made his own pronouncements on the subject of Armageddon and the end of the present 'system of things', as the Watchtower translates the word, *aionos*, age. His first pronouncement was that Jesus came in 1897: 'Our Lord, the appointed King, is now present, since October 1874' (*Studies in the Scriptures Vol. 4*, p. 62), and that the end of the world, Armageddon, would take place in October 1914. Russell engaged in a complex set of calculations that fixed the date. According to the Watchtower, the Fall of Jerusalem took place in 607 B.C., although it actually took place in 586 B.C. It then goes to Daniel Chapter 4, describing the fall of Nebuchadnezzar, who was deprived of his sanity and throne and became as a beast of the field for seven years. The Watchtower takes these seven years to have a prophetic sense, rather than simply referring to Nebuchadnezzar, and makes the following calculations, in addition to the ones he made using pyramidology:

> The seven years were equal to 84 months, or, Scripturally allowing 30 days for each month, 2,520 days. At Revelation 12:6, 14, 1,260 days are mentioned and described as 'time, times and half a time', or 3½ times. 'Seven times' would be twice 1,260, or 2,520, days. Ezekiel, a faithful prophet of Jehovah, wrote, 'I have appointed thee each a day for a year.' (Ezekiel 4:6). If this rule is applied, the 2,520 days become 2,520 years. Therefore, since God's typical kingdom with its capital at Jerusalem ceased to exist in the fall of 607 B.C, then, by counting the Gentile times from that date, the 2,520 years extend to the fall of 1914 A.D.
> *Let God Be True,* pp. 245-246

This is perhaps one of the most blatant misuses of the Scriptures by the Watchtower. It is hardly necessary to comment on the background to the various texts it uses in the most arbitrary fashion, but its misuse must be confronted. Yes, Revelation 4:6,14, does mention 3½ years, but this does not have any relevance to the figure juggling in which the Watchtower is indulging. In the Book of Revelation's symbolism, it merely means a short period of time, not the fullness of time that 7 years (the perfect number) would represent. Ezekiel 4:6 refers to a command of God to the prophet to lie down on his side for a set number of days to bear the sins of the nation of Israel, one day representing a year of its sins. It does not establish a rule that every day should represent a year.

1914

So to begin with, it was not the year 1914 that Russell heralded as the beginning of Armageddon, but its ending. The 'seventh trump' was supposed to have sounded in 1840, then Christ was supposed to have come in 'the character of a Bridegroom in 1874' (*The Watchtower, October 1879,* p. 4*)*, or alternatively 1872 or 1873, to begin taking his power and beginning to reign.

What was meant to happen in October 1914? According to the Watchtower, Armageddon and the end of the world. In the years running up to this date *The Watchtower* and *Awake* magazines were replete with 'prophesies' of approaching Armageddon, and the Jehovah's Witnesses were constantly being urged to be prepared, to sell even more copies of the organisation's publications, to be even more zealous in spreading Watchtower doctrines. However, when October 1914 came and went without Armageddon, the Watchtower had to begin backtracking. The 1/11/1914 issue of *Watchtower* stated that, 'Studying God's Word, we have measured the 2,520 years, the seven symbolic times, that year 606 B.C. (sic), and we have found it reached down to October 1914, as nearly as we were able to reckon. We did not say positively that this would be the year.' (Of course, it positively had said that it would be).

As the First World War progressed, which did indeed begin in 1914, the organisation began to teach that the war was the beginning of the overthrow of the earthly systems and that it would take place in 1915 instead, and then in 1918, continually moving the goalposts as the months progressed.

'Invisible presence of Christ'

When it was obvious that Armageddon had not happened and with disillusioned members drifting away, the Watchtower had to come up with an alternative. This alternative was to be the invisible presence of Christ. According to the Watchtower, although Jesus went to heaven after his Resurrection as Michael the Archangel and sat on his throne, it wasn't until 1914 that Jesus began to reign as King. 'After his death, Jesus was resurrected and went to heaven. There, he waited for God to say when it would be time for him to start ruling as King of God's Kingdom' (*pamphlet, The Government that will Bring Paradise,* p. 19), and references below, giving the reference Psalm 110:1), which of course simply says, 'The Lord says to you, my lord/ Take your throne at my right hand, while I make your enemies your footstool'. This verse does not say anything at all about Jesus having to wait nearly 1900 years to reign as king in heaven.

When Jesus took his seat at God's right hand on his throne after his Ascension, then he was straight away reigning as King. Of course, he always was King, although, as he said to Pilate, his Kingdom is not of this world. After his Ascension Jesus began to rule in his glorified body until 'he has put all his enemies under his feet' (1 Cor.15:25) The Watchtower then details what happened as Jesus now reigns: he casts Satan out of heaven, he begins to rule, and the Watchtower says this is proved by wars, food shortages, diseases and earthquakes, with men ruining the earth. Then, Jehovah's Witnesses began telling the 'good news'.

When the Jehovah's Witnesses came round one morning they began talking about this 'invisible presence'. I had just returned from Mass and pointed out that they need only go down the road to the Catholic church and they would have there the presence of Christ in the Eucharist that had been with us for two thousand years. Jesus promised to be with us until the end of time (Matthew 28:20), and he has been with us in the Eucharist, in the sacraments, in the Church, in other people, in ourselves in the divine indwelling. We didn't have to wait for 1900 years! – If we had not had his divine presence with us in the Church for 2,000 years, then Jesus was lying to us.

1925

The Watchtower also 'prophesied' new dates. Keeping to their insistence of the dates, 1914, 1918 (the downfall of Christendom and Christianity and the destruction of churches), the Watchtower then added a Jewish harvest time of forty years. In the book, *Millions Now Living Will Never Die,* (pp. 89, 90), published in 1920, written by the successor of Charles Taze Russell, who died in 1916, 'Judge' Rutherford prophesied that in the year 1925 the 'worthies' of the Old Testament, as he designated them, Abraham, Isaac, Jacob and other faithful ones of the Old Testament would be resurrected 'and fully restored to perfect humanity and made the visible, legal representatives of the new order of things on earth'. 'There can be no more question about 1925 than there was about 1914' Rutherford declared. 'This chronology is not of man, but of God,' added *The Watchtower* magazine. 'Being of divine origin, present-truth is absolutely certain. (15/7/1922, p. 217). Rutherford therefore ordered the construction of a palatial, landscaped, 10 roomed, Spanish mansion, Number 4440, Braeburn Road, San Diego, California, to house his distinguished visitors. He named it *Beth Sarim*, 'House of the Princes'. When they sadly failed to turn up, Rutherford blamed the Witnesses, saying, 'The difficulty was that the friends inflated their imaginations beyond reason; and that when their imaginations burst asunder, they were inclined to throw away everything' (*The Watchtower 1925* p. 262).

It was typical of the Watchtower officials to blame their followers rather than themselves.

Rutherford did not allow his imagination to burst asunder, though, even though it was he who had thought the idea up; neither was he inclined to throw everything away, and moved into the mansion himself. He described this situation in his book, *Salvation,* p. 311:

> [T]he purpose of acquiring that property and building the house was that there might be some tangible proof that those on earth today who fully believe in God and Christ Jesus and in His kingdom, and who believe that the faithful men of old will soon be resurrected by the Lord, be back on earth and take charge of the visible affairs of earth. The title of Beth-Sarim is vested in the WATCHTOWER & BIBLE TRACT SOCIETY in trust, to be used by the president of the Society and his assistants for the present, and thereafter be for ever at the disposal of the aforementioned princes on the earth.

The property was sold in 1948, so another false prophecy came to nothing. Not until after Rutherford had given it a new twist, though. Barbara Grizzuti Harrison[21] describes how she attended the 1950 Convention in the Yankee Stadium. Fred Franz, the Society's vice-president, made a solemn announcement, 'The princes are here in our midst, among us tonight!'

A fearful hush came over that stadium', when Franz dropped his bombshell I

---

[21] *Visions of Glory* (New York, Simon & Schuster, 1978), p. 181.

felt a quick stab of disbelief, followed immediately by flutters of guilt, and then by overwhelming anxiety. Franz paused for maximum effect, as thousands gathered in the dusk shifted restlessly in their seats, craning to see – what? Did any of us believe that Solomon would step before the lectern? '*You*,' Franz cried anticlimactically, 'are the princes'; and he explained that Jehovah had shed greater light on his word, and the princes were not, as we had for so many years believed, the 'faithful men of old', but congregational overseers, whom God was grooming for positions of authority in his New World. There was great and fervent applause, as if a dream had been fulfilled, and not mercilessly deflated. I was very angry.'

However, Franz added, this would take place only when paradise earth had been established. It was another nail in the coffin of her disillusion with the organisation that led her to leave it and return to her Catholic roots.

1975

The Watchtower then came up with yet another date to which its followers could look forward, with a different set of calculations, and this was 1975. This time, the Watchtower estimated the number of years from the creation of Adam. The Watchtower accepted the order of creation literally, but the length of a creation day figuratively, and according to its calculations one day is seven thousand days long. The whole creation process then took 49,000 years. I go to the explanation given by W.C. Stevenson[22]:

> It is based upon the assumption that the length of the seventh day, the Sabbath, can be calculated. Since it is assumed that God has not created anything or anybody since man, He is therefore presumed to be still resting from His creative work. In other words, the seventh day, or Sabbath, is still in progress. By starting at the year 539 B.C, which is claimed to be the absolutely proved year in which Cyrus, King of Persia overthrew the Babylonian Dynasty, and working backwards through the Old Testament by means of its various chronological records, the Witnesses have arrived at the year 4026 B.C. as the date for the creation of Adam. It is therefore roughly 6,000 years since the creation of Adam in Eden. Since the Witnesses believe that in this generation the millennium, the thousand year reign of Christ is due to begin, we must therefore add another 1,000 years to the already elapsed 6,000, giving us 7,000 years in all as to the length of the seventh day. If the seventh day is 7,000 years long, then it is reasonable to suppose that all the other six days are of the same duration.

---

[22] *The Inside Story of the Jehovah's Witnesses* (New York, Hart Publishing Company, 1967), pp. 70,71

It is on such flimsy and ill-founded suppositions that in the 1950s the Watchtower determined that the end of the world would now take place in 1975 and promoted the date relentlessly. 'After almost 6,000 years of human sorrow, suffering and death, at last permanent relief is near at hand and will be realised within this generation' (*New Heavens and a New Earth, 1953,* p. 7). Young members were discouraged from marrying or from going on to further education, many Witnesses sold their houses and property, many people took low paid jobs in order to give more time to the Watchtower. Then as usual, profound disillusionment set in as 1975 came and went and the Watchtower had to revise its calculations under the guidance of 'new light', as ever blaming everything on its followers:

> It may be that some who have been serving God have planned their lives according to a mistaken view of just what was to happen on a certain date or in a certain year. They may have, for this reason, put off or neglected things that they otherwise would have cared for. But they have missed the point of the Bible warnings concerning the end of this system of things, thinking that Bible chronology reveals the specific date.
> *The Watchtower 15/7/1976,* p. 440

In *The Watchtower 1/4/1972*, p. 197, the Watchtower said, 'Does this admission of making mistakes stamp them [Watchtower] as false prophets? Not at all, for false prophets do not admit to making mistakes.' (No, false prophets are those that prophesy falsely.) Since it always seems to blame its followers, not itself, then the assumption again must be that it is a false prophet.

Since then, although the Watchtower continues to tell its followers that Armageddon is just round the corner, soon, within 'this generation', it has lengthened the odds by the simple expedient of discovering that we don't know how old Adam was when he was driven from the Garden of Eden, or when Eve was created, so 'this generation' can happily be prolonged.

Prophecy or teaching?

When I started to bring up these conflicting and false 'prophecies' with a Jehovah's Witness, he said that teaching develops, that, in the terminology of the Watchtower, 'new light' had been shed on the subject. I agree that doctrine can develop, as it has in the Catholic Church, but not changed completely. However, these dates and the teachings connected with them did not start out as teaching but as prophecies. The Bible says that if a prophecy fails to materialise then the one who prophesied is a false prophet. Of course, some Biblical prophecies have not yet taken place and will be fulfilled in the future, but the Watchtower 'prophecies' had specific dates attached to them and they most definitely failed to materialise. As the Watchtower itself states, correctly:

> The three essentials for establishing the credentials of a true prophet, as given through Moses, were, The true prophet would speak in Jehovah's name; the things foretold would come to pass (Deuteronomy 18:20-22); and his prophesying must promote true worship.
> *Insight on the Scriptures Vol 2, 1988,* p. 696

Did the Watchtower claim to speak in the name of Jehovah? The organisation, as we have seen, puts itself forward as the 'faithful and discreet servant' which is God's sole, true mouthpiece on earth, so we can say that it did. However, it denies that it did so:

> Jehovah's Witnesses, in their eagerness for Jesus' second coming, have suggested dates that turned out to be incorrect. Because of this, some have called them false prophets. Never in these instances, however, did they presume to originate predictions 'in the name of Jehovah'. Never did they say, 'These are the words of Jehovah.'
> *Awake! 22/ 3/ 1993*, p. 4

This is an interesting quotation. Firstly, it blames its followers for falsely predicting Jesus' second coming, when it was the Watchtower alone that published, predicted and promulgated the dates. Jehovah's Witnesses are forbidden to put forward teachings of their own. It also blames its followers for being accused of being false prophets, but it was the organisation itself, and it alone, that falsely prophesied. No, perhaps its followers did not say, 'these are the words of Jehovah', or presume to originate predictions, but the organisation itself did make that claim:

> So God's servants know what this world's rulers do not. They know Jehovah's purposes and his seasons.... Since Jehovah's servants of today obey him as ruler, God's holy spirit also reveals to them what season it is from his viewpoint.
> *The Watchtower 1/5/1938* p. 143

> Who will be Jehovah's prophet to the nations, to speak to them everything that He should command? Who will be the modern Jeremiah?... Back there, about forty years ago, that was the question. Today we may ask, how was the question answered? There are facts to show. We should not appeal to religious pride or boasting or self-made claims. We should appeal to the facts. Let the facts speak for themselves.... Whom has God actually used as his prophet?... Jehovah's Witnesses are deeply grateful today that the plain facts show that God has been pleased to use them.
> *The Watchtower 15/1/1959*, pp. 40, 41

If the Watchtower Organisation can so easily be proved to be a false prophet, then we can confidently say that it is not of God. Indeed, there is an intriguing sentence in *Studies in the Scriptures* (the forerunner of the *Watchtower* magazine), Vol. 7 p.128 that says, 'No doubt Satan believed the Millennial Kingdom was due to be set up in 1915'. So the Watchtower is saying here that it was actually Satan who was behind the 'prophecies'.

Still, even now, Jehovah's Witnesses eagerly await Armageddon, which they are constantly being told will be 'soon', so now we need to examine to what they are looking forward.

CHAPTER 17

ARMAGEDDON

When you meet a Jehovah's Witness it will not be long before he will speak of Armageddon. It is true to say that Jehovah's Witnesses live, eat, drink and die expecting Armageddon which, with the prospect of living afterwards in paradise earth, is at the heart of their religion and of all they do for the Watchtower Society.

The name appears in Revelation 16:16: 'they [the demonic spirits of v.14] then assembled the kings in the place that is named Armageddon in Hebrew.'

Armageddon (Megiddo) was the scene of some decisive battles in the Old Testament – Judges 5:19-20, 2 Kings 9:27, 2 Chronicles 35: 20-24, so it was natural that St John saw it as symbolic of the decisive rout of the forces of evil.

The Watchtower interpretation

The name Armageddon means the Mountain of Megiddo, but since there is no mountain nearby, only a mound rising above the adjacent valley plain, the Watchtower says that it signifies a condition or a situation,

A Catholic Response to the Jehovah's Witnesses

in this case symbolic of a global war fought against God. Also, because all the kings of the earth will be gathered together for the battle the plains of Megiddo would be too small to hold them all, so it must be symbolic. (If the section (vv.14, 16) has to be interpreted literally, it says that the kings, (now, mostly Presidents and other rulers!) not their armies, are being assembled, so the Watchtower has to include Revelation 19:19 in its scenario to make it a worldwide battle). What of the battle?

It is Satan and this present evil system of things that is under his control – that is, the entire secular world and every religion other than the Watchtower – that will be totally destroyed. For this reason Jehovah's Witnesses look forward to this time when Satan and evil, including all who are not Jehovah's Witnesses, will be destroyed. Here are just a few quotations from Watchtower publications:

> That battle will put out of existence all the wicked angels together with Satan, the Devil, and all the humans who are serving this wicked organisation.
> *God's Way is Love,* p. 28

> It will destroy Satan and all his agents – [by 'agents' the Watchtower includes every secular institution: schools, hospitals, every political system, every religious organisation except the Watchtower].
> *This Good News of the Kingdom,* p. 23

> What comes to an end is the wicked world ... bringing destruction to Satan and his wicked demons. Christ Jesus will lead the heavenly hosts of Jehovah's in this final

> attack against Satan and his organization, destroying it utterly.
>
> *ibid.,* p. 25

> This will be Jehovah's fight in which all wickedness will be swept from the universe … it will completely destroy the invisible and visible parts of Satan's world
>
> *Let God be True,* p. 259

We need to emphasise that when the Watchtower says that 'all humans who are serving this wicked organisation will be destroyed, it does mean everyone who is not a Jehovah's Witness, including babies and young children. It speculates that even children of Witness parents may not be spared if they have not had time to 'earn' their redemption. 'Only Jehovah is capable of waging a truly just and truly selective war during which righthearted individuals, wherever they may be on earth, will be preserved.' (*Jehovah Witness website – A Happy Beginning*).

During the battle, which will be between the armies of heaven and earthly armies, the Jehovah's Witnesses will take no part. The Watchtower calls on the battle under Jehosophat in 1 Chronicles 20:15 – 24 to illustrate this:

> The battle of Armageddon is over, every single human being has been destroyed, except those Jehovah's Witnesses who have been actively working for the organization on earth at the time. Now Paradise Earth has arrived.

Now begins Paradise Earth.

CHAPTER 18

PARADISE EARTH

To live for ever on a paradise earth is a central tenet of Watchtower faith and one of its most distinctive doctrines. Jehovah's Witnesses believe in a paradise earth, a promise of future happiness that their organisation offers to prospective converts, and the hope to which the Witnesses continually look forward and which fills their thoughts and aspirations.

First of all, where does the phrase 'paradise earth' come from and what does it mean?

The phrase 'paradise earth' appears nowhere in the Scriptures although *paradise* does. The Watchtower defines it as:

> In the Greek *Septuagint* version of the Bible the translators appropriately used the term 'paradise' with reference to the garden of Eden, because it evidently was a closed park. After the account in Genesis, Bible texts that tell about paradise refer to (1) the garden of Eden itself, or (2) the earth as a whole when it will be transformed in the

future to a condition like that of Eden, or (3) flourishing spiritual conditions among God's servants on earth, or (4) provisions in heaven that remind one of Eden.
Reasoning From the Scriptures, p. 284

The Watchtower sees it as Eden restored at the beginning of the 1000 years of the Millennial reign of Jesus in heaven, and that will continue after his final return for the 'great crowd' of only Jehovah's Witnesses and those who through the thousand years have been reconstituted, or as the Watchtower would phrase it 'resurrected', been given a second chance, and have then accepted Watchtower teachings.

Although the Watchtower professes to abhor all shreds of paganism within Christianity, the word 'paradise' itself is of pagan, Persian origin, meaning a pleasure garden. It appears three times in the Scriptures:

Paradise in the Scriptures

Luke 23:43
'Amen, I say to you, today you will be with me in Paradise.'

The NWT renders this as 'Amen, I say to you today, You will be with me in Paradise,' because, as we have seen, it believes that Jesus – and all of us – cease to exist on death, so Jesus could not say to the penitent thief that he would be with him that day in paradise. It is the only version as far as I know that renders it in this way.

There is another consideration: the Watchtower says that Jesus would not be on paradise earth, but ruling from heaven, so even its rendering contradicts its own teachings.

If the NWT is correct, why did Jesus need to say he was speaking to the thief 'today'? That was perfectly obvious! It would have been a waste of precious, dying breath for Jesus to say so. What Jesus did promise was that the thief would be in 'hades' 'Abraham's bosom' as it is variously described, that abode where the souls of the just who died before Jesus' coming were waiting for him. Jesus had not at that point ascended to heaven, but would be going down to the world of the dead, to those righteous men living before the time of Christ who were awaiting his coming. This is where the man will be, temporarily, with them (1 Peter 3:19, 20). Heaven would be fully opened only after Jesus had risen from the dead on the third day.

On one visit a Jehovah's Witness denied Jesus' saving grace to Adam, although there is no biblical text that denies the fruits of the Resurrection to Adam and Eve. They also denied heaven to all those born before his resurrection, including John the Baptist. I quoted the following passage from what the *Catechism* describes as an 'ancient homily for Holy Saturday':

> Today a great silence reigns on earth, and a great stillness. A great silence because the King is asleep. The earth trembled and is still because God has fallen asleep in the flesh and he has raised up all who have slept since the world began.... He has gone to search for Adam, our first father, as for a lost sheep. Greatly desiring to visit those who live in darkness and the shadow of death, he has gone to free from sorrow Adam in his bonds and Eve, captive with him. He is both their God and the son of Eve (CCC 635).

When I quoted this ancient text the Jehovah's Witness proudly said that they did not depend on human authors but on the Bible, disregarding the voluminous Watchtower publications they have to read and believe in. However, this is an important text, because it shows several things:

- From the earliest times the Church has interpreted texts such as 1 Peter 3:19, 20 as affirming Jesus' descent into Hades to bring up with him into heaven all those who had 'fallen asleep' in the hope of resurrection before his death and resurrection.
- Unlike the Watchtower, which reserves heaven for 144,000 and paradise earth to Jehovah's Witnesses only, the Church has always seen the redemption and salvation won for us by Jesus on the Cross as offered and available to *all*, from Adam onwards. The Church knows, unlike the Watchtower, that only God knows who are in heaven.
- It affirms that from the earliest days, the Church acknowledged the divinity of Christ: 'God had fallen asleep', as well as his humanity 'son of Eve'.
- The text uses the phrase 'fallen asleep', which is often used in the Scriptures, and which we have discussed in an earlier chapter, and does not mean oblivion or annihilation.

2 Corinthians 12:2- 4
'[I] was caught up into Paradise and heard ineffable things which no one may utter.'

St Paul said that he was caught up into the third heaven (of Paradise): Therefore, the earthly paradise of Eden has now been 'translated' into heaven. It is no longer on earth. It was also not the fullness of the heavenly vision.

Revelation 2:7.
'I shall give them to eat of the tree of life, which is in the paradise of God.'

This could refer back to the tree of life in Eden, but some scholars think it could also be a reference to a tree in the temple of Artemis at Ephesus, where there was a right of refuge for asylum seekers and which John used as an illustration for the Christians of the far greater and truer reward that awaited them.

Therefore, there is nothing in the Scriptures that describes it as the earth as a whole when it will be transformed in the future to a condition like that of Eden, or flourishing spiritual conditions among God's servants on earth, or provisions in heaven that remind one of Eden.

Permanence of paradise earth

The reason why the Watchtower insists on a paradise earth is because it believes that the earth is permanent. There are several texts that it uses to 'prove' it. Its favourite one is Psalm 37:29: 'the just will possess the land [NWT 'earth'] and live in it forever'. The argument is that if the just will live in the land forever, then it must be permanent.

The Psalm is referring to the land of Israel, not the earth. (there is only one word, *eretz* for both land and earth). I pointed out to a Jehovah's Witness that the psalm is poetry and does not have to be taken literally, but to no avail.

Another text is Matthew 5:2, 'Blessed are the meek, for they will inherit the land,' which a Witness quoted to me, without averting to the fact that verse 8 says 'Blessed are the clean of heart for they will see God'. Of course, the Watchtower is emphatic that the ordinary Witness, however pure, however clean of heart he may be, will never see God, so why should they give a literal interpretation to verse 2?

It is strange that the Watchtower gives to the earth a permanency that it does not give to the human being and even to the person of Christ without it first being annihilated and then reconstituted.

New Heavens and New Earth

However, Scriptural texts do speak of the destruction of the earth and the cosmos, and a new heavens and a new earth coming into being. The main text for this is 2 Peter 3:10, 12, 13:

> But the day of the Lord will come like a thief, and then the heavens will pass away with a mighty roar and the elements will be dissolved by fire, and the earth and everything done on it will be found out ... hastening the coming of the day of God, because of which the heavens will be dissolved in flames and the elements melted by fire. But according to his promise we await new heavens and a new earth in which righteousness dwells.

This is apocalyptic language, but destruction is assumed, to make way for a new heavens and a new earth, in which the whole universe will be transformed by the reign of God's righteousness and justice. (cf. notes in NAB)). Revelation 21:1-3 sees heaven being wedded to earth in indissoluble unity under God's reign:

> Then I saw a new heaven and a new earth. The former heaven and the former earth

> had passed away, and the sea was no more. I also saw the holy city, the new Jerusalem, coming down out of heaven from God, prepared as a bride adorned for her husband. I heard a loud voice from the throne saying, 'Behold, God's dwelling is with the human race. He will dwell with them and they will be his people and God himself will always be with them [as their God].

This is not the vision that the Watchtower has and which it offers to its followers. God will not be with his people in the Watchtower paradise earth, but governing through the worthies of the Old Testament on earth. What the Catholic faith offers to us is that total union with God, where he dwells with us in a life of unimagined love, glory and peace. However, it does envisage that Creation will share in this transfigured life, just as it shared in the Fall:

> The whole creation is eagerly waiting for God to reveal his sons. It was not for any fault on the part of creation that it was made unable to attain its purpose, it was made so by God; but creation still retains the hope of being freed, like us, from its slavery to decadence, to enjoy the same freedom and glory as the children of God (Romans 8:19–22).

Beginning to live on paradise earth

The Watchtower's ideas of paradise earth contain many contradictions and inconsistencies. To begin with, as they enter paradise earth and the 1,000 reign of Christ begins in heaven, those Witnesses alive after Armageddon will begin the task of clearing up after the slaughter, burying the bodies of the dead. At the time of writing there are some six-seven million Witnesses in the world, and over six billion people, so these Witnesses have the job of burying six billion bodies – and rising. The Watchtower estimates that it will take the Witnesses about eight months to accomplish this, a very optimistic estimate! They will then have to start rebuilding the destroyed infrastructure and this will take them the next thousand years to complete.

Conditions on paradise earth

During the '1000 year reign 'He [Jesus] will gradually take sin away from our minds and bodies.' So during the '1000 year reign' the paradise earth will be imperfect, and sin is still there. 'There will no more sickness, old age and death. Old persons will become young again' – but how can they become young again if there is no old age? The people will have to work to make the earth a paradise, rebuilding the ruined infrastructure. How long will that take and where and how will they live while doing so?

'Millions of dead will be resurrected to human life on earth.' The reference is to Acts 24:15, which says there will be a resurrection of the righteous and the unrighteous (no mention of this being during the 1000 year reign). Since there will be billions of dead people by then, how will the small proportion of the millions be chosen, and why will this be some of the unrighteous? If the unrighteous are resurrected to the 'paradise earth' how can this be paradise? for presumably they will still be at liberty to reject the Watchtower teaching which they will be obliged to study.

Will this be an immediate judgment? The text gives time for them to 'do' what God requires of them, which implies a time scale, and also that they are still free not to do what was required of them, in other words, to sin against God. How does all this differ from life on earth now? Then, where will the wicked be 'removed' to during the 1000 years.

Watchtower publications show a paradise earth, with smiling people of all nations, animals living in harmony; lush vegetation, not a factory or house in sight. The implication is that this is what everybody yearns for, a world with no sickness, no death, no pain. A Jehovah's Witness asked me, in amazement, why I didn't want to live on paradise earth. When I described some of these reasons why not, but above all because Jesus would not be on paradise earth, he responded that this was how the Watchtower imagined it. Precisely! But it is supposed to be the reality to which the Witnesses aspire and in which they must believe. In fact, it is mostly the imagination of Judge Rutherford. This is how he imagines it:

> The New World, moreover, will be a diseaseless world; for the curative powers of the Divine Physician will be turned towards this earth (Matthew 4:23; Psalm 103:2, 3). Aches and pains will die out, as radiant health, unmarred by cancer, or influenza, or even toothache, implants itself in every soul (Revelation:21:4) this means the dissolution of old age, with its wrinkled skin, its gray hair, and feebleness. It means that vigorous energetic youth, so fleeting today, shall be the eternal lot of every human. To enjoy these blessings perpetually necessitates the removal of man's greatest enemy, death.
> *Let God be True,* p. 263

It is understandable that people yearn for this outcome, and it is one of the most potent prospects that the Watchtower can offer to people. However, would we really like to live eternally, for ever and ever, on earth, doing all the things we do now, although without the pain, hardships and decay that we have now? Is there not the possibility that we would eventually become bored? Especially when we will not have there the most precious thing that we already have, as firstfruits, here on earth, the presence of God?

Christ no longer present

Christ will no longer be even an invisible presence on the earth, so this paradise earth is poorer than Eden, when God 'walked and talked' with Adam and Eve. This paradise earth is also far poorer compared to what we as Catholics have even now, before our death, where we have the presence of Christ in the Eucharist and in the sacraments; in his presence in the Church; in the indwelling of the Father, Son and Holy Spirit within us; when we already have the down payment of eternal life in the sealing of the Holy Spirit; where we are already living at every moment in the presence of Christ. We have the hope given to us by Jesus Christ himself that we shall be in his presence for all eternity. What a poor exchange the Watchtower paradise earth is!

Where is the devil?

We learn that Satan and his demons will be put out of commission, locked away in an abyss of inactivity during the Thousand Year Reign of Jesus Christ. No longer

will those malicious creatures be lurking behind the scenes, fomenting trouble and trying to goad us into acts of unfaithfulness against God. (Rev 20: 1-3)
Knowledge that Leads to Everlasting Life, p. 183

This text says that Satan will be 'imprisoned' for a thousand years, but other Watchtower texts say that he will be **destroyed** prior to the 1000 years.

A Catholic response to the 1000 years.

Many Christian sects and denominations believe literally in the 1000 year reign of Christ on earth; however, although a literal translation was widespread in the Early Church, this was ultimately rejected. The Church has traditionally interpreted it differently, bearing in mind that the Book of Revelation uses symbols, which are not be taken literally. She therefore sees it as referring to the age of the Church, either beginning from the Resurrection of Christ, or the end of the Roman persecution of Christians, (see JB note b) when satan is restrained, held at bay, by the sacraments. The thousand years stands for the time Christ would reign through the Church, bearing in mind that the thousand years is also symbolic, simply meaning a very long time. At the end of time there will be a final confrontation when satan will be crushed once and for all.

Why was the earth created?

A Jehovah's Witness started off one session by asking whether I agreed that the earth was made for man. I said, no; the Scriptures say that earth was created for Jesus and by and through him (Colossians 1:16). My response was that the primary purpose of Creation was that it was created for Jesus. It is a reflection of his visible glory. Jesus is the fulfilment of all creation. He is the *real* vine, the *true* bread. All material creation is but a shadow of the reality that is in Christ in heaven. All will find their fulfilment in him. Creation shares in our redemption, just as it shared the consequences of our sin: 'creation itself would be set free from slavery to corruption and share in the glorious freedom of the children of God.' (Romans 8:21).

The Witness dismissed that perfunctorily, and insisted that the earth was also made for man in the second place, to which I agreed, although the Witness's intention was to say it was the primary purpose. This is another example of a point of doctrine that I had not thought of before, and which the Witness had brought up that I needed to explore further. Thinking over why I felt that there was something wrong with the Watchtower teaching, I realised that Scripture says that although earth was created for Jesus, it was *given* to man. Why does this distinction matter?

The Watchtower insists that earth was made for man because it considers that this supports its teaching on the permanency of earth, because Jehovah's Witnesses will live forever. However, if we follow the teaching of Scripture that the earth was *given* to us, then it emphasises that we, too, are part of creation; that we, too, are made for Christ. We are put on earth as its custodians, 'to till it and to keep it', and that it shares in our sin just as it shares in our redemption, but it will not remain in its present state, just as we will not remain in our present state.

Creation is important, because God created it, for his honour and glory, and he has a glorious destiny for it. When the Scriptures say that 'the earth will endure forever, it does not necessarily mean that it will remain in its present, earthly form, although the Watchtower insists it will. As we have seen, 2 Peter 3:10, says that the heavens will pass away with a mighty roar, and the elements will be dissolved by fire, and the earth and everything done on it will be found out (or be burnt up). Verse 13 then says that 'we await new heavens and a new earth in which righteousness dwells (Repeated in Revelation 21:1). This is God's promise. (The Jehovah's Witnesses at this point interpret earth figuratively, as meaning 'wicked human society').

New Heavens and New Earth

Revelation: 21:1.
Then I saw a new heaven and a new earth. The former heaven and the former earth had passed away, and the sea was no more, there are no longer mountains and islands (Revelation 6:20)

Whenever the Scriptures talk of a new earth, it always speaks of new heavens. This new heaven and new earth, in the Scriptures, does not come, as the Watchtower teaches, after Armageddon, but after the Second Coming of Christ and the end of time.

The Watchtower interprets the 'new heaven and new earth' as the 'new heaven' being the organisational rule of Jesus /Michael the Archangel and the 144,000.

Our belief, though, is in this new heavens and new earth. Just as we are redeemed, so our earth shares in our redemption. Earth is united with heaven and is subsumed into heaven. In fact, this has already happened in the Incarnation of Jesus Christ, who, as the Son of God took on our human flesh, uniting heaven and earth in his own person. In Jesus, heaven has already come down to earth. To a certain extent we, too, have already begun to share in this as he has made us partakers of his divine nature even here on earth, while we await its fullness in heaven. (2 Peter 1:40).

So what is the fulfilment of all that God in Christ had achieved for us, that is, the Kingdom of Heaven?

CHAPTER 19

KINGDOM OF HEAVEN

There is a chapter in *Let God be True* that describes the Watchtower understanding of what the Kingdom of Heaven is like, and Catholics might well be startled at how different it is to what they have been taught.

In John 18:36ff Jesus speaks of 'my kingdom'. Is this different from the Kingdom of Heaven?

The Watchtower says that Jesus became king only in 1914. But Jesus said 'the Kingdom of God is among you' (Luke 17:21). This is sometimes translated as 'The Kingdom of God is within you', and the Watchtower is correct that 'among you' or 'in your midst' (NWT) is more accurate; although *'entos'* does mean 'within', *'umon'* you, is in the plural. The Watchtower then goes on to say, 'Jesus who was in their midst, thus referred to himself as a future King. Far from being something that a person has in his heart, God's Kingdom is a real, operating government having a ruler and subjects.' (*Knowledge that Leads to Everlasting Life,* p. 91).

This explanation is very misleading. Jesus is actually saying that the Kingdom of God is already present, because he is already present in their midst; he is not pointing to himself as a king in the future and therefore a kingdom in the future. He is speaking in the context of the Pharisees asking what the signs of the coming of a future kingdom are, and Jesus is saying they should not do that because the kingdom is already present, the exact opposite of what the Watchtower is interpreting this passage as saying. Further, when Jesus stands before Pilate he affirms that he is a king (present tense), and that his kingdom is not of this world (he already has a kingdom, he does not have to wait until 1914).

What is more serious is the Watchtower's dismissal of God's presence within the human heart. Although the verse of Luke 17:21 strictly speaking does not speak of God within us, John's Gospel certainly does. At the Last Supper, and therefore on the most solemn and serious of occasions, Jesus gives his unequivocal promise of the Divine Indwelling in the hearts of his friends: 'Whoever loves me will keep my word, and my Father will love him, and we will come to him and make our dwelling within him.' (John 14:23). To St Paul this was such a glorious reality that one of his favourite expressions was 'God in you' (e.g. Colossians 1:27), which is our hope of glory (*ibid.*).

The Watchtower, of course, diminishes this rich understanding by rendering it as 'Christ in union with you, the hope of [his] glory'. (NWT). By inserting 'his' into this verse, the Watchtower is denying that his glory is also ours, because St Paul says that we 'All of us, gazing with unveiled face on the glory of the Lord, are being transformed into the same image from glory to glory, as from the Lord who is the Spirit' (2 Corinthians 3:18). In all the Watchtower literature I have read, I can see no understanding of this transformation into the image of Christ as the aim and the goal of Christian life.

The Kingdom as organisation

What, then, is the Watchtower concept of the Kingdom of God? It is purely an organisational replacement for the human, earthly governments destroyed at Armageddon, 'a real, operating government having a ruler and subjects'. 'Judge' Rutherford even describes Jesus as 'the Great Executive Officer of Jehovah God' (*Salvation*, p. 326). In the Watchtower heaven, Jesus as King rules with the reconstituted 144,000 from heaven over the Jehovah Witness subjects on paradise earth. Since Jesus, or as he is in Watchtower teaching now, Michael the Archangel, is a spirit being, as are the 144,000, they will all have to have earthly representatives on earth who have a hotline to these heavenly spirit rulers. As we have seen, according to the Watchtower these will be the patriarchs and worthies of the Old Testament, who were supposed to return in 1925 and for whom the mansion at San Diego in California, was prepared.

Of course, Jesus does acknowledge that he is a king, and after his Resurrection says that 'all power is given to me in heaven and on earth', (Matt 28:18). Compare Daniel 7:13-14 where one 'like a son of man' is given power and an everlasting kingdom by God. The risen Jesus here claims universal power. He then took his place at God's right hand in heaven after his ascension into heaven.

The Richness of the Kingdom of God

Reading the Watchtower's ideas about the Kingdom of God, it is difficult not to feel how weak and unsatisfactory it is compared what Jesus himself says of it. Many of Jesus' parables are about the kingdom of heaven, and he compares it to a pearl of great price, a precious coin lost by a housewife, a sower sowing seed in the ground, a field sown with wheat and tares, a tree where the birds could roost, a vineyard, a king going off to a far country. There are so many vivid similes and illustrations. The Kingdom of God is multi-faceted, a growing, organic thing that cannot be limited to just one concept of a government with a ruler and his co- rulers in heaven, and the ruled on earth below.

Reading Watchtower literature, I cannot help being struck by how legalistic both the Watchtower organisation is, and its understanding of what the Kingdom of God, is, and, indeed, its whole belief structure. In *Visions of Glory,* (page 17) Barbara Grizzuti Harrison quotes a remark of Hayden Covington, describing the beginnings of the world in the garden of Eden: 'It was a legal matter. The [forbidden] tree served as a legal sign, a guidepost between God-King and man in their governmental dealings with each other. Adam and Eve failed to fulfil their contract. It is a contractual, not an ecstatic, religion'. There is here no sense of that intimate friendship between God and his beloved, created, son and daughter with whom he talked and walked in the Garden of Eden and from whom he asked for their loving, freely given obedience.

I feel this is true of the whole Watchtower structure and belief. Although it talks about love in its publications, and relationship with Jehovah God, I cannot help feeling that life as a Jehovah's Witness is more about obeying the rules and directives of the Watchtower organisation than nurturing a loving, filial relationship with God our Father, made visible in Jesus Christ and made active through the outpouring of the Holy Spirit of Love into a person's being.

PART 4

INSIDE THE ORGANISATION

You might still be interested in inviting a Jehovah's Witness into your house and to find out more about their teachings. What will happen if you want to find out how to join their organisation? In the next section we will explore the Watchtower and how it is organised. What I describe and the information I give is from books and literature of those who have attended Jehovah's Witnesses meetings, as I have not myself attended any of them.

CHAPTER 20

BECOMING A JEHOVAH'S WITNESS

There is a knock on the door and two Jehovah's Witnesses are standing there. They will perhaps ask you what you think of a current world situation or say that they would like to share a verse from the Bible with you. You think that what they are saying is interesting, perhaps resonating with your own dissatisfaction with how things are going in the country and the world; perhaps you feel unhappy with the Church. The Witnesses say that they have a more optimistic message for you and a real Christian organisation that will teach you what the Bible really teaches, rather than the false teachings of your own Church. You invite them in and they talk about the Bible and perhaps introduce into the discussion their belief of a new world order just round the corner. You are sufficiently interested to agree to their suggestion that they come round for further discussion and agree to a six week Bible study course. This is likely to be based on one of their newest publications, '*What Does the Bible Really Teach?*'

The Kingdom Hall

After six weeks, if the Witnesses feel that you are sufficiently open to what they have been teaching you, they might invite you to come to attend a service at their Kingdom Hall the following Sunday and you agree. At one time groups met once a week in people's houses for Bible Study on Tuesdays, but this has now been discontinued. Your arrival will have been carefully planned for; a Witness will come with you, so that you will not have to come to an unfamiliar meeting on your own. Everyone will be most friendly to this newcomer; you notice that they address each other as 'brother' and 'sister'.

Kingdom Servants

You will be taken round to meet the 'kingdom servants', the local officials who run the meetings and the business of the Kingdom Hall. There is the congregation servant who is in charge of the local organisation. The assistant congregation servant is responsible for collecting all the reports of the house to house visits, compiling the statistics and sending a monthly report to the branch office.

The magazine-territory servant deals with the supply of literature to the members and distributes the Watchtower magazines *The Watchtower* and *Awake!* He is also responsible for the territory file. This is a map in which the district assigned to the congregation is divided up into sections of about three hundred houses, and it is the responsibility of the magazine-territory servant to allocate to the members the area they will visit on a rolling programme.

The literature servant is responsible for the books, pamphlets and Bibles that the Witnesses use in their work.

The *Watchtower* study conductor takes the study of the Society's official journal in the Sunday meetings, and the Ministry School Servant is responsible for the midweek training school, which is described below. The Watchtower organisation, even at the local level, is highly organised and regulated.

Keeping records

You will see a notice board on the wall that gives the figures for Witness activity – numbers of books and literature sold or placed in households, numbers of houses visited, the number of back visits and Bible studies held, and you are impressed with the zeal of these people who are so eager to share their faith. However, although members are required to do some form of house to house visitation, the amount of time expected for ordinary members has dropped from ten hours a month to a quarter of an hour, so all is not is as it seems.

Looking round, you notice that the Kingdom Hall is nothing like the church you are accustomed to – no altar, no Blessed Sacrament, no candles, no flowers. It is more like a meeting room with a podium and a lectern, and when the meeting begins that seems to be what it is; it is nothing like the Mass you have been accustomed to.

Kingdom Hall Meetings

A Catholic, Kenneth Guindon, who for a time became a Jehovah's Witness describes his first visit to a Kingdom Hall. As they were told to stand for the opening prayer Kenneth automatically raised his hand to make the sign of the Cross, and hastily remembered where he was. He found the 'dry question-and-answer format' rather boring.

Although the meeting began and ended with a song, the Witnesses do not call them hymns, and the ones they use are specific to them; he didn't really feel he had been at church, worshipped God or prayed, because, of course, he hadn't been!

Maybe you will feel the same, but the warm welcome you received will encourage you to go again. For the Bible study, you will be given a copy of the week's *Watchtower* magazine, and a copy of their *New World* Bible; the Bible study will be based on the subject given in the magazine. A Witness may proudly tell you that all over the world every Witness is studying exactly the same thing. You may recall that at Mass the same Scripture Readings are also being read in all the Catholic Churches all over the world. One difference is, though, that the priest is free to prepare his own homily on the Scripture readings, but the Witnesses are given no such freedom.

You notice that there are questions at the bottom of the page of the Watchtower magazine you are studying; the Witnesses who respond to the question and answer format put their responses in their own words, as they are encouraged to do, and which reinforces the Watchtower teaching, but they stick strictly to the answer that is given in the relevant paragraph. They are not encouraged to put their own thoughts about the subject. Indeed, although they will allow you to put your own point of view while you are an interested newcomer, if you later become a Jehovah's Witness you will be allowed no such freedom and could be disfellowshipped if you do so.

More Meetings

You continue to go to the Sunday meetings, because you think that you are learning quite a bit about the Bible, even though it is so different from what you heard at Mass, and after a few weeks you are invited to other meetings at the Kingdom Hall.

You study the latest publication issued by the Watchtower, and these books, too, are based on the question and answer format, with questions for each paragraph at the bottom of the page and the answers contained in the paragraph above. Although it is considered Bible Study you may not be aware that it is not like Bible study groups that meet in some Catholic parishes. These may study a theme – faith, for example- or perhaps go through a book of the Bible. But in the Witness Bible Studies what you are really doing is studying what the Watchtower teaches with Bible quotations given (often with no real connection to the text), to support the teaching.

Arrangements are made for the week's house to house visits which last for up to three hours at a time. As you become more involved, you will find that you will be expected to prepare for the Sunday meeting by going through the week's *The Watchtower* first, looking up the references; you soon find out that there are quite a few more meetings that Witnesses are expected to attend.

The Theocratic Ministry School, followed by the Kingdom Service School meets on Thursdays, to train Witnesses in all aspects of their work, in public speaking and good speech. As you progress in your involvement you will be invited to attend these extra meetings, and you might find these Thursday meetings very helpful. You might not have been accustomed to public speaking but once you have enrolled in the school you will be expected to give an eight minute talk to the assembled Witnesses. Your performance will be marked and criticism and encouragement given, and you might find that it boosts your confidence. This can be very encouraging to new enquirers as they learn these new skills

Going Door to Door

You find that Service School is quite fun, too, because it involves role play and sketches on how to do house to house visiting and how to respond to the householders they meet. Soon, you will be encouraged to put all this into practice and come on a house to house visitation yourself. They assure you that you won't have to do anything yourself, for you will be with an experienced Witness and all you need to do is look and listen. You might find it quite interesting and even fun, although mostly you will be met with rejection. But that doesn't matter, because by now you will know to expect that from Satan's evil organisation, that is, any person who rejects your message. And after your training in Watchtower doctrines and Bible study methods, you are likely to feel quite superior to those who do invite you in and you realise how little they know about the Bible compared to the Witnesses.

Preaching Statistics

However, you will find that it is also difficult work, trying to persuade people to join the Watchtower, which can be dispiriting. In 2007, for example, Witnesses spent 1.4 billion hours in educational work such as door to door witnessing and Bible Study groups, carried out by 6,957,852 members, with 298,304 new members baptised, although, of course many join but are not baptised (*Authorized site of the Office of Public Information of Jehovah's Witnesses*). In the booklet *'Jehovah's Witnesses, Who are They?* P. 26, published in 1997, it says, 'Jehovah's Witnesses spend over 1,000,000,000 hours a year proclaiming the good news, and more than 300,000 new ones are baptized.' This means that over 3,000 hours are spent to gain one convert, but this figure does not account for children baptised from Witness families, so the number of hours needed for one adult convert would be even higher. *jwfacts.com* states that 'Due to the high rise in people leaving, the number of hours preaching required per additional publisher increased between 1991 and 2005 from 4,000 to 16,000, an increase of 400%!' You will no doubt be impressed at the zeal of the Witnesses willing to put in so many hours for one person, but you could find it daunting as you carry on going from door to door with such little success.

Separation from the World

By now you are very much involved with all the Jehovah's Witness activity and the friends you are meeting. You hardly notice that you have so little time left that previous friendships are dropping by the wayside. Besides, you are absorbing more and more the understanding that all those outside the circle of the Jehovah's Witnesses are destined for destruction at Armageddon, and are all part of Satan's evil organisation, so it is not advisable to make oneself part of that world. Indeed, you are more and more encouraged to distance yourself from them, except when you can witness to your new faith and show them the error of their ways. At home, this can cause some friction, unless members of your family can be persuaded to follow in your steps.

Coming from a Catholic background you may find that your Catholic relatives and family are very upset, but you have been so well trained that you are easily able to refute their arguments. Besides, you are being taught that the Catholic Church is the worst of all Satan's organisations so that by now you are perhaps only too willing to separate yourself from them.

Baptism

Until now you have become an unbaptised Witness, attending meetings, doing door to door ministry, but now you are ready to take the final steps towards being a fully-fledged Jehovah's Witness. You are ready to be baptised at one of the Conventions, which can be at the district, regional or national level, which is held once a year. Once there, you are exhilarated to find yourself part of this enthusiastic crowd of hundreds or even thousands of people all united in a common faith, so well-behaved and well-organised, (no dropped rubbish left behind!) and are happy to become fully one of them.

You find that the Watchtower baptism is not at all like your Catholic baptism, although, if you have been baptised as a baby, you won't remember it! But you have probably attended Catholic baptisms. The Witnesses explain that your baptism will not be that of being 'born again' (John 3:5-8) as Jesus promised, you will not be baptised into the death and resurrection of Jesus Christ to rise with him to newness of life, (Romans 6: 1-11) as you were when you were baptised as a Catholic; the Watchtower baptism applies only to the 144,000 whom the Watchtower designates as the 'holy ones' who 'share the Kingdom with the Son of man, Jesus Christ'. (*Reasoning From the Scriptures,* p. 56). Of course, no matter how holy you are, as a Jehovah's Witness you are not destined to inherit the Kingdom of Jesus Christ in heaven any longer, only a paradise earth.

Watchtower baptism will not cleanse you from sin; quoting 1 John 1:7, 'If we walk in the light as he is in the light, then we have fellowship with one another, and the blood of his Son Jesus cleanses us from all sin' the Watchtower explains that it is only the blood of Christ that cleanses from sin. According to the Watchtower, Matthew 3:11 and Acts 13:24, which speak of a baptism of repentance, refers only to the Jews, as does Acts 2:38, in which only that the Jews present 'now put their faith in Jesus as the Messiah, the Christ'. (*Reasoning from the Scriptures,* pp. 55, 56). Again, this argument is specious; the Church gives us the Scriptures because in it all that the Gospel offers and invites us to embrace is for all. It may be that Jews were the first audience and the first Christians, but the promise is for everyone.

The Watchtower does not explain how the blood of Christ is applied for the forgiveness of sins, because this does not happen at their baptism. In Catholic teaching we receive the cleansing from sin through the blood of Christ at our baptism, we receive it in the Sacrament of Reconciliation and when we participate in Christ's sacrifice for us on the Cross at every Mass.

Watchtower Baptism

What, then, does your baptism as a Jehovah's Witness signify?

> Water baptism is a requirement for all who want to have a relationship with Jehovah God. Baptism publicly indicates your desire to serve God. It shows that you are delighted to do Jehovah's will (Psalm 40:7, 8). To qualify for baptism, however, you must take definite steps.
> *What does the Bible Really Teach?* p. 175

These steps and undertakings are then set out.

You undertake regular attendance at meetings in order to increase accurate knowledge of God's will, acceptance of Watchtower teachings you have learnt so far, sharing your faith with others, leading a moral life. Of course, this is what every baptism should entail, but the problem is that the Watchtower leeches out of the baptism itself the power and the grace of God that will enable those submitting to Christian baptism to live in that newness of life.

> 'Going beneath the water symbolizes that you have died to your former life course. Being raised up out of the water indicates that you are now alive to do the will of God. Remember, too, that you have made the dedication to Jehovah God himself, not to a work, to a cause, other humans, or an organisation. Your dedication and baptism are the beginning of a very close friendship with God – an intimate relationship with him (Psalm 25:14).
> *What Does the Bible Really Teach?* p. 183

Catholic Baptism

There is much that a Catholic can agree with in this definition. In Catholic baptism we, too, die to our old life to rise, not only to be alive to do the will of God but to share in the Risen Life of Jesus Christ, which includes doing the will of God. Our Catholic baptism also is 'the beginning of a very close friendship with God – an intimate relationship with Him', but note that the Watchtower baptism only *symbolises* a death and resurrection. In contrast, St Paul, and the Church, sees it as something very real: 'are you unaware that we who were baptized into Christ Jesus were baptized into his death? We were indeed buried with him through baptism into death, so that, just as Christ was raised from the dead by the glory of the Father, we too might live in newness of life.' (Romans 6:3, 4). The reality of our baptism is just as real and transforming as the death and resurrection of Christ himself. Following St Paul's teaching the Catholic Church sees baptism as:

> the basis of the whole Christian life, the gateway to life in the Spirit, and the door which gives access to the other sacraments. Through Baptism we are freed from sin and reborn as sons of God; we become members of Christ, are incorporated into the Church and made sharers in her mission (CCC 1213).

Life as a Jehovah's Witness

You will not find things very much different after your baptism, although if you are a male you will be encouraged to aspire to being a congregation servant, and if you are single you will be encouraged to become a full-time publisher.

One of the things you may very well find is that when the Watchtower has said 'Remember, too, that you have made the dedication to Jehovah God himself, not to a work, to a cause, other humans, or an organisation. Your dedication and baptism are the beginning of a very close friendship with God – an intimate relationship with him', this does not exactly represent the reality of your new life. You are now dedicated to a cause, which is to spread Watchtower teachings and the work of the organisation. It is true, Catholics also, by their baptism, are incorporated into the Church, because they become part of the family of God, and by your Watchtower baptism you are dedicated to the Watchtower organisation, but you will find that the two realities are very different.

Perhaps you will indeed find that it is the beginning of a very close relationship with God, but many converts find that this is not the case. With so much work to do, especially if you work full-time for the organisation, Watchtower activity leaves you with very little time for the quiet times of prayer that are necessary to cultivate your relationship with God. Indeed, the organisation actively discourages you from seeking that intimate relationship and growth in prayer and union with God because it actively discourages you from cultivating anything that is not controlled by the organisation.

So what happens if you eventually become disillusioned with the Watchtower and wish to leave?

CHAPTER 21

LEAVING THE WATCHTOWER

In some ways it is difficult to leave the organisation, because if you have been in it for some time you will have lost your former friends and now the only friends you have are in the organisation. As well, you have been so indoctrinated to consider anyone outside the Watchtower as belonging to Satan's realm that there will be that deep feeling that if you do leave you will lose your salvation. And what if the destruction of Armageddon is true and it will happen in your lifetime? Many Witnesses say, 'where will we go to?' It's a scary feeling. Many Witnesses testify that they stay on for many years after they no longer believe in the Watchtower and its teachings, and even continue to preach to others what they no longer believe themselves.

There is the realisation that once you do leave you will be cut off from all the Witnesses you once knew, who will no longer speak to you, you will be, in the Watchtower terminology, 'shunned'. If there are family members who are Witnesses then they, too, will no longer be allowed to consort with you on pain of being disfellowshipped themselves. In a family situation in the same home communication is still acceptable. So it is a very serious step to take.

Some statistics

Despite that, though, the Watchtower has the highest rate of those leaving of any other religious body. The Watchtower itself says that it disfellowships 1% of its members a year. With its membership around 6 million, then that means that it disfellowships some 6,000 members a year, of which perhaps a third are later reinstated. Then there are those who still attend meetings but do not engage in active door to door work, those who drift away. In 2005 41% left the organisation. Since the Watchtower keeps very precise records, its figures can always be checked on the Internet.

Reasons for leaving

Why do people leave the Jehovah's Witnesses? After prophecies prove untrue; for example in 1914, 1925 and especially 1975, when the Watchtower had predicted Armageddon, many people became disillusioned and left. Now, the organisation is careful not to put exact figures on things. Many people leave when 'new light' is shed on issues, which means, not a development in doctrine but a reversal of what had been taught before. Many start reading the Scriptures for themselves without Watchtower publications to interpret, and they find that what the Scriptures say is far different from what the Watchtower teaches.

You might start questioning those teachings; you might find yourself becoming increasingly disillusioned with the fact that you are required to believe that everyone is doomed to destruction at Armageddon, apart from active Witnesses. If you start flagging in your zeal from going door-to door, or missing meetings, you might find yourself being ostracised for being of 'bad attitude', and might be warned that this will jeopardise your assurance of being saved at Armageddon.

Although you have been told that everyone, apart from committed Jehovah's Witnesses, will be destroyed at Armageddon, when you go from house to house you meet so many good people, so many committed Christians who are alive with the love of God, so many good people who are not believers. Perhaps you start thinking that surely God does not want them destroyed. And anyway, when will Armageddon arrive?

Again, you might come to be increasingly concerned that the Witnesses engage in no active work apart from preaching. Although individual Witnesses can be very generous in helping other Witnesses, there are no structures within the organisation itself to do this, and you feel it is not right that your commitment to Christ will not allow you to reach out in compassionate action to the poor, the sick, those in any kind of need, while you are a Witness. You may question why this is so, and we will discuss this issue next.

CHAPTER 22

NOT OF THIS WORLD

On one visit, the Jehovah's Witnesses came into my living room and I heard one of them murmur something about goats, presumably because he had seen the crucifix on the wall. Using- and misusing - the parable of the sheep and the goats of Matthew 25:31-46, the Watchtower divides everyone into sheep (Jehovah's Witnesses) and goats (those outside the organisation and destined for destruction), who refuse to accept the message of the Jehovah's Witnesses.

By using the parable in this way totally ignores the real import of the parable, in which Jesus divides people into sheep, those who serve and minister to him by feeding the hungry, clothing the naked, visiting the prisoner, and those who do not. The Watchtower must interpret the parable in some other way, because it is adamant that it is not for the Jehovah's Witnesses to engage in social action of any sort, because their sole purpose within the organisation is to preach the Watchtower doctrines. Any activity which takes a Witness away from 'Kingdom' business is frowned upon.

Young Jehovah's Witnesses leaving school are discouraged from going on to higher education, because, with Armageddon so near, pursuing a career is a waste of time and exposing them to 'the world', the devil's evil system of things. Rather, they are encouraged to become full time publishers for the Watchtower organisation. Most Witnesses have poorly paid jobs, in order that they are freer to devote themselves to Watchtower work.

Watchtower work is to Publish

The Watchtower does not engage in social work of any kind, because the only work of the Jehovah's Witnesses is to 'publish', that is, to promulgate Watchtower teachings. To the question, 'Why don't you people get involved in doing things to help make the world (the community) a better place to live?' the Witnesses are given the following explanation to respond:

> Why do you feel that this has become such a major need? Obviously, immediate action on the matter can be beneficial, but I'm sure you'll agree that we would like to see improvement on a long-term basis. That is the approach that we as Jehovah's Witnesses take to the matter. (Explain what we do to help people to apply Biblical principles in their lives in order to get to the root of the matter on a personal basis; also, what God's Kingdom will do, and why this will permanently solve the problem for humankind).
>
> Another possibility: Some do it by establishing institutions - hospitals, homes for the elderly, rehabilitation centres for drug addicts, and so forth. Others may volunteer to go right to the homes of

people and offer appropriate help as they are able. That is what Jehovah's Witnesses do.

Reasoning From the Scriptures,
pp. 207, 208

In other words, all that the Witnesses offer is tell people about a future paradise on earth, and no attempt is made to make the lot of people easier here and now, or to hasten God's kingdom by reaching out to those in need and showing them the love and compassion of Jesus. Because there is such a short time before Armageddon, the Witnesses are told, it is more important to spread Watchtower teaching. Apart from the fact that Armageddon is not just round the corner, and much good work could have been done by the Witnesses in the 150 years or so of the organisation's existence, Jesus himself gave us an example; he had a public ministry of only three years, yet managed to combine his preaching and teaching with a ministry of healing and, from the group's purse that Judas kept, ministered to the needs of the poor. This is something that the Church has done ever since, following his example and his command.

No distractions from Publishing

Another reason for this lack of care for any outside their organisation, is that to run institutions or projects to help those in need would take the Witnesses away from their only occupation which is not only to promulgate Watchtower teachings but also to sell its publications. Bear in mind that the full title of the organisation is Watch Tower Bible and Tract Society. It is not a Church or even a sect as such, but a publishing house. Its vast real estate, especially in America, is funded by the sales of its books and magazines that are distributed all over the world. Witnesses have to take the weekly magazines that they will study at their meetings, but with changes in the law, and to preserve their charitable status, they no longer ask for a donation or payment for their books, leaflets and magazines when they go from door to door. This has meant a reduction in their finances and has meant the selling off from some of their real estate and combining some printing operations, relying even more on their members for funding.

Because the Watchtower considers every human institution as belonging to the evil system of things ruled over by the Devil, Witnesses are forbidden to salute the flag in America, belong to a political party or even to vote. They will be grateful to a policeman if they are victims of a crime, for example, but are forbidden to work as a policeman themselves, because that will be working for an evil organisation in this 'system of things'. However, they do take advantage of what the Devil's system offers, such as health care, education, benefits, etc. None of this is provided by the organisation itself. Individual members are often generous in helping fellow Witnesses. I must say, though, that when a Witness was coming to my house each week and I was not well she offered to do shopping for me. I gratefully declined, though, as my husband was able to do it. The help given to other Witnesses is usually limited to those described as 'in good standing'. Those who are not actively involved in house to house preaching are often not included.

What happens when you are 'not in good standing', that is, have disobeyed Watchtower rulings or sinned in some way?

CHAPTER 23

DISFELLOWSHIPPING

If you go to a Watchtower meeting you might perhaps notice that although there is great friendship and warmth among the 'brothers and sisters' there might be someone sitting at the back of the hall, not joining in with the discussions or the role playing, not being asked to give a presentation, if he is a man. No-one speaks to him or approaches him. He is disfellowshipped and must be shunned, which is one of the most disturbing practices of the Watchtower Organisation. There might be others who come just before the meeting starts and leave immediately it finishes, without staying for the refreshments afterwards. These are people who are 'marked', that is, not disfellowshipped but under warning, as it were.

The practice of disfellowshipping derives from what St Paul says in 1 Corinthians 5:2-5. It concerns a man who had committed incest, and Paul says that he should be expelled, or as the Church expresses it, excommunicated, from the community. Delivering the man to Satan means that once he is expelled from the Church, the sphere of Jesus' lordship and victory over sin, he will be once again in the region where Satan is still master. The aim is for him to be brought back into repentance and reunion with the community.

In one sense this is also the aim of disfellowshipment, but the practice is far more extreme than ever St Paul envisaged. The person disfellowshipped is allowed to attend meetings, but not permitted to participate in any way, lest he contaminate the rest. At home, if it is a Jehovah's Witness family, he may talk to other members of the family about ordinary matters, but not allowed to speak of Watchtower matters. Outside the family, no Witness is allowed to speak to him, and even other Witness family members might shun him. People have spoken of the anguish this brings to families torn apart: parents not allowed to attend their children's weddings, grandparents no longer allowed to see their grandchildren.

Given that a Witness's life is totally controlled and bound up with the organisation, and that by now he has no friends in the outside world, this can be an intensely lonely and frightening experience. However, one Witness said that strangely she found it a liberating experience, because sitting at the back, listening what was being said, gave her a detachment and a distance that enabled her to assess things dispassionately and that enabled her to make the journey out of the organisation into the Christian faith.

What can cause someone being disfellowshipped? Apart from moral issues, immorality, witnesses can be disfellowshipped for smoking, for questioning any of the organisation's doctrines; attending a funeral, a wedding or any other service in a Christian Church; reading non-Watchtower religious books or magazines. One full-time publisher said that he was threatened with disfellowshipping when, becoming bored with preaching time after time the talk given to him by the Watchtower, he gave a talk of his own on the Lord's Prayer. Witnesses can be disfellowshipped for speaking to one who is already disfellowshipped or has left the organisation.

The Watchtower keeps meticulous records of its membership, and these records show that a fairly consistent 36,000 Witnesses are disfellowshipped a year, and of these about 24,000 are readmitted. This means that some 12,000 members are dismissed from the organisation a year.

Number disfellowshipped annually - 1.00%

This is based on *The Watchtower 1/7/1992*, p.19:

> "In recent years disfellowshippings worldwide have been approximately 1 percent of publishers." *The Watchtower 1/1/1986,* p.13 stated, "It is to be noted, also, that during the past year, 36,638 individuals had to be disfellowshipped from the Christian congregation" In 1985 average publishers were 2,865,183, so 36,638 represented 1.28%.
>
> "Unfortunately, during the 1986 service year, 37,426 had to be disfellowshipped from the Christian congregation..." Of the 3,063,289 publishers this represented 1.22%.
> *The Watchtower 15/91987,* p.13

Number reinstated - 0.33%

I have used an average figure of 1/3 of the number disfellowshipped subsequently being reinstated. This is based on the following comments.

> "36,671 persons had to be disfellowshipped for various kinds of serious wrongdoing. Yet, in that same period 14,508 persons were reinstated..." This equates to 39.6% being reinstated.
> *The Watchtower 1/8/1974*, p. 466

> "During the service year of 1958-1959 there were 6,552 individuals disfellowshiped by the New World society of Jehovah's witnesses for various reasons ... and there were 1,597 ... Reinstated..." This equates to only 24%. (Taken from the website *jwfacts.com*).
> *The Watchtower 1/12/1960*, p. 728

The figures for 2018 were: baptisms 281,774, an increase of 111612. However, this increase was offset by those missing 170162, died, 70116, became inactive 45602, which led to a debit of 4106 on those baptised and cut the increase to 7506. This does not include those disfellowshipped, for which I couldn't find figures, apart from the site saying that 5443 were not disfellowshipped.

The harsh attitude towards the world outside the Jehovah's Witnesses continues to be insisted upon in order to deter members from leaving:

> Because of listening to the Devil and not rejecting his lies, the first human pair apostatized. So, then, should we listen to apostates, read their literature, or examine their Web sites on the internet? If we love God and the truth, we will not do so. We should not allow apostates into our homes or even greet them, for such actions would

make us 'sharers in their wicked works'. May we never succumb to the Christian 'path of truth' to follow false teachers and who seek to 'introduce ruinous ideologies' and try to 'exploit us' with well-turned phrases.

The Watchtower 15/1/2006, p. 3

Leaving the Watchtower

Despite these warnings, what happens when you start flagging, when the doubts begin to trouble you, when you start to miss meetings, when you start to question the teachings or be guilty of some other wrongdoing?

You can simply drift away, which many do. Some stop coming to meetings, but when events in the outside world give cause for concern – the financial crash of 2008, for example, many come back, just in case Armageddon really is just round the corner.

The decision to disfellowship a member is made by a meeting of three elders and announced to the local meeting. You are then no longer a Jehovah's Witness.

CHAPTER 24

THE WATCHTOWER AND WAR

One of the topics that the Jehovah's Witness will almost invariably bring up is the question of war, which they oppose. The Witnesses are not pacifists, though. Although no-one in the armed forces is permitted to become a Jehovah's Witness, and no Witness is permitted to join the armed forces, they look forward with eager expectation to Armageddon and that War to end all wars with all the bloodthirsty descriptions furnished for them by the Watchtower imagination!

A Jehovah's Witness said to me that none of the early Christians were soldiers, but this is not true. I pointed out that when soldiers came to John the Baptist to ask his advice he tells them to be content with their pay, not to give up their day job. Jesus heals the centurion's servant, and commends his faith, Peter is sent to a centurion to baptise him. There is no evidence that they were told to give up their position, and many of the early Christian martyrs were soldiers. The reason why it became difficult for Christians to serve in the army was because of the oath they had to swear to the Emperor as a god and give him unconditional obedience; this was incompatible with their oath of allegiance to Jesus. There is no condemnation of the career of the soldier as such in the New Testament. Of course, a Christian can be just as against war as any Witness, and it is not necessary to become a Witness in order to be a pacifist.

It is easy for the Watchtower to point out truthfully that Christian has been fighting against Christian for many centuries, and say that therefore they are not true Christians:

> For example, Jesus said of his followers: 'They are no part of the world, just as I am no part of the world' (John 17:14). However, many professed Christians are deeply involved in the political affairs of this world, even being involved in bloody wars. Rather than conform to Bible standards, many people would wish the Bible to conform to their own standards.'
> *The Watchtower 15/12/1996*

This can easily put us on the defensive. However, some points can be made.

The Watchtower was not always against war, but gradually became so between the two World Wars. In 1898 it said there was no prohibition against military service:

> Notice there is no command in the Scriptures against military service. Obedience to a draft would remind us of our Lord's words: 'If any man compel thee to go a mile, go with him twain.

> The government may compel marching or drilling, but cannot compel you to kill the foe. You need not be a good marksman.
> *Zion's Watch Tower*, 1/8/1898, p. 231

During the Second World War Witnesses were encouraged to buy American war bonds to help the war effort.

The Watchtower says that unlike the Churches, Jehovah's Witnesses spoke out against Nazism. An *Awake!* article of 22/8/1995 states that after the Watchtower convention in Berlin 25 June 1933 in which some 7,000[23] assembled to draft "a declaration of the Facts" to state their case to Hitler, persecution came upon the Witnesses. However, this declaration which the Witnesses sent to Hitler is reproduced in the 1934 Year Book of Jehovah's Witnesses and in fact supports the Nazi regime:

> The greatest and the most oppressive empire on earth is the Anglo-American empire. By that is meant the British Empire, of which the United States of America forms a part. It has been the commercial Jews of the British-American empire that have built up and carried on Big Business as a means of exploiting and oppressing the peoples of many nations.... The present government of Germany has declared emphatically against Big Business oppressors and in opposition to the wrongful religious influence in the political affairs of the nation. Such is exactly our position... Instead of being against the principles

---

[23] The declaration states that 5,000 were present, not 7,000.

> advocated by the government of Germany, we stand squarely for such principles.[24]

It seems that the Watchtower's hatred of capitalist and communist regimes, the Catholic Church, as well as Christian denominations, was so great that it was willing then to speak out in support of a regime that fought against them, regardless of the heinousness of the Nazi regime.

It is true that a few days after the Watchtower issued the above document, quoted in part above, a copy of which was also sent to Hitler himself, Witnesses and their leaders were rounded up and thrown into concentration camps. The Nazi regime was unconvinced by the Watchtower's support and knew enough of the organisation to know that its members would refuse to fight in the army, and was against all secular powers. It is also true that at the beginning Witnesses were subjected to even greater brutality than other prisoners, and showed heroic courage, with many being killed. However, the Nazis soon realised that while the Witnesses would refuse to fight they would also not resist the regime in any way, and their treatment became much more benign, with Witnesses often put into trusted positions as servants. I pointed out that if everyone had taken such a passive stand against the Nazis, then it is likely that the Third Reich would not have been defeated.

The Witnesses are rightly proud of their brothers and sisters martyred by the Nazis, but we, as Catholics, can also be proud, as well as sad for the thousands of martyrs, bishops, priests, religious and laity, as well as for every group and every individual, who were also killed under the Third Reich, as well as six million Jews. Indeed, Hitler's hatred of the Church came only second to his hatred of the

---

[24] The full text of this letter is given in Appendix 2.

Jews, and his plan was not only the eradication of all Jews, but then the eradication of the Catholic Church.

Non-pacifists

During a visit, a Witness may give the impression of being totally pacifist, and, of course, a Catholic can be against war, can be a pacifist, too. It is an individual choice, although the Church supports the principal of the just war. Just as an individual has the right to defend himself, his property and those who depend on him, so a state has the right to defend its citizens against attack. However, an article entitled 'Wars That God Blessed' in *The Watchtower 1/10/2010*, shows that the organization does defend war in certain circumstances:

> Ancient Israel, a nation uniquely chosen by God centuries before Christianity was established, was at times authorized to assemble an army and engage in warfare. Before entering Canaan, the land that God had promised to Abraham, the Israelites were told: 'Jehovah your God will certainly abandon [seven nations] to you, and you must defeat them. You should without fail devour them to destruction. You must conclude no covenant with them nor show then any favour.' (Deuteronomy 7:1, 2). Thus, Israelite General Joshua defeated those enemy nations 'just as Jehovah the God of Israel had commanded. (Joshua 10:40).
>
> Was this a ruthless conquest wherein Israel greedily subjugated foreign countries? Not at all. Those nations had become full

of idolatry, bloodshed and degraded sexual practices. Even children were killed in sacrificial fires. (Numbers 33:52; Jeremiah 7:31). God's holiness, justice, and love for God's people compelled him to remove all uncleanness from the land. Even so, Jehovah searched the hearts of everyone – and spared those who were willing to abandon wicked ways and serve him.

This passage raises interesting questions. The Watchtower condemns fighting against the Nazis in the Second World War, but how can it think that the death of millions, not just of children, but men women, gypsies, Catholics, Protestants, homosexuals, the disabled, the mentally ill, the Jews above all and, of course Jehovah's Witnesses, in the gas ovens, fires and torture chambers, did not warrant God authorising the nations to take arms to battle against those horrors?

The Watchtower says, correctly, that there were Christians fighting against Christian on both sides, both claiming that God was on their side. Of course there were Christians on both sides, because there are Christians in every country. In the above passage from the Scriptures, the Watchtower acknowledges that there were good men on both sides and yet God still authorised the battle.

Pope Pius X11

The Jehovah's Witnesses will also inevitably bring up the usual tired lies about Pope Pius X11 first spread by Rolf Hochut in his play 'The Representative' Until then, the Pope was widely revered for his work in saving Jews during the War. It is estimated that some 850,000 Jews were saved by his intervention in various ways – instructing religious houses in Italy to shelter them, hundreds sheltered in the Vatican, many men inducted into the Swiss Guard to give them immunity, hundreds given false passports and documents, hundreds sheltered by Italian families, etc. He was not silent during the War; he was the author of *Mitt Brenennde Sorge*, before he became Pope, but issued in the Pope's name, a document issued from the Vatican against the Nazi regime, but he decided not to speak out publicly after that. He saw that when the Dutch Archbishop did speak out, as a result all Dutch Jews and Jewish Christian converts were rounded up to go to their deaths, and he could not risk that happening elsewhere. Surely the number of lives saved was more important than making statements! Einstein, in the United States, wrote an article to say that the Catholic Church had saved more people than any other organisation. I don't know whether The Watchtower issued any statement condemning the Nazi regime, but I haven't seen any literature to that effect myself.

There is now abundant literature available on what the Catholic Church did on behalf of the Jews, countering the falsehoods and opening its archives, so be confident that you can give a robust response to the Witnesses if you do your homework.

CHAPTER 25

BLOOD TRANSFUSIONS

Most people know that the Watchtower forbids blood transfusions. Quite recently, there was an item in the papers when a young man who had been involved in a serious accident, refused to have a blood transfusion that would probably have saved his life. The Kingdom Servant responded to journalists' questions by saying that it was the young man's decision, following his conscience. However, the young man's conscience was formed by Watchtower teachings. What is the reasoning behind these distinctive teachings which were introduced into the organisation in 1944? Its justification for them is the Biblical prohibition against eating meat with the blood still in it. The main text is Leviticus 17:11,14:

> Since the life of a living body is in its blood, I have made you put it on the altar, so that atonement may thereby be made for your own lives, because it is the blood, as the seat of life, which makes atonement.

> You shall not partake of the blood of any meat. Since the life of every living body is its blood, anyone who partakes of it shall be cut off.

There is also Genesis 9:4 – Only flesh with its lifeblood in it you shall not eat.

The ruling of the Council of Jerusalem described in Acts 15: 28, 29, enjoins Christians 'to abstain from things offered to idols and from blood and from things strangled'.

Neither Judaism nor the Church has interpreted these texts as forbidding blood transfusions, and neither has the Church forbidden Christians from eating non-kosher meat, that is, meat from which the blood has been drained, despite the prohibition of the Council of Jerusalem. Further, it seems that Witnesses are not obliged to avoid meat which has not been drained of blood, which was the purpose of the original prohibition.

If the Watchtower interpretation is correct, it has, and has had, serious consequences, because Witnesses, and the children of Witnesses, have been allowed to die rather than disobey the Watchtower's rule.

Alternative interpretation

In what way can we as Catholics approach the Scriptural texts? From the context of the Old Testament texts, it refers only to animal meat, and not cannibalism, the eating of human flesh, which would never have entered their minds. They refer to animals killed in hunting, but also, and even more, to ritual sacrifices. These ritual sacrifices have been made obsolete by the death and resurrection of Jesus, the true Lamb of God who shed his blood on the Cross, (cf. Hebrews 9 and 10) and therefore the prohibition is also obsolete for Christians. Catholic and Orthodox Christians now partake of the sacred Body and Blood of Jesus Christ, which is why St Paul tells the Corinthians that that they are not to participate in pagan rituals (1 Corinthians 10).

With reference to the instructions of the Jerusalem Council, the early Christians were faced with two problems. One was the Judaizers, who wanted the Christians to follow the Mosaic Law, and the other was the pagan environment where meat sacrificed to idols was sold in the shops and markets.

The Christians and Jewish converts in the regions of Antioch, Syria and Cilicia, with large Jewish populations, had asked the Apostles to look into the issue, as they were coming under pressure to obey the Mosaic Law. The Apostles made it plain that Christians were no longer obliged to follow the Mosaic Law. That it was not meant as a universal command can be seen from 1 Corinthians 10:18-31, which sheds light, not only the Mosaic prohibition, but also the question of meat sacrificed to idols. It is a question of freedom and conscience. St Peter had already had his vision described in Acts 10, when God had said that the Mosaic dietary laws no longer applied, and now St Paul starts from the same basis. The Christian cannot share in pagan sacrifices, but they need not worry about eating the meat from pagan sacrifices being sold in the market, except if it disturbed their own or someone else's sensitivity. They should eat what is put before them unless it causes offence to other Christians, which obviously means that they could be eating meat with the blood in it.

Inconsistencies in the Watchtower prohibitions

The Watchtower acknowledges that the Biblical texts forbid the *eating* of blood, which of course does not apply to blood transfusions, which is the infusion of a bodily organ. Although the Watchtower forbids blood transfusions it now accepts the components of blood, or blood products like albumin, (Erythropoietins), vaccines, immunoglobulins, and hemophiliac treatments, and said that "...when it comes to fractions of any of the primary components, each Christian, after careful and prayerful meditation, must conscientiously decide for himself." Since 1 December 2000 the DPA (Durable Power of Attorney) a legal document signed by Jehovah's Witnesses in the USA, had been amended to allow member to accept the previously forbidden fractionated blood parts.[25]

However, after so many years of absolute prohibition, it is not easy for individual Witnesses to make that decision for themselves, and I wonder how many of them realize that there is this loophole. Also, it is difficult to understand how individual components of blood can be acceptable, but not those components when combined as a whole.

The Watchtower 15/6/2000, p. 29-31.

It seems that since the year 2000 the Watchtower stance has begun to change, because in a statement to the European Commission on Human Rights it said that there are no "controls or sanctions" for a Witness who accepts blood and that minors may not carry "Advance Medical Directives", and it admitted that it was no longer disfellowshipping members who accepted blood or prohibited blood components. Are their members aware of this?

In the 5/6/2000 *Watchtower*, Questions From Readers, an article opened the door to the use of hemoglobin since it is fractionated from red blood cells. So it seems that

---

[25] Trevor Willis, *Can Jehovah's Witnesses Survive?* (Kindle edition), location 3815

the organization seems is be easing its policy and may eventually abandon it altogether.

The question remains; how will the Watchtower sell this to its members, after so many years when this has been such a visible sign of the organization? There have been so many times when it has successfully changed its doctrines with the slogan of shining 'new light' on the Scriptures, but this is surely one of the most significant. The Watchtower literally has blood on its hands with the deaths of members who have died rather than go against this Watchtower injunction and it must surely give rise to great anger and disillusion once this change in policy becomes more widely known to its membership.

PART 5

CATHOLIC PRACTICES UNDER FIRE

When the Jehovah's Witnesses found that they could not persuade me by their arguments they often then begin to attack the Catholic Church. They have plenty of material to go on, from the Crusades, the Inquisition, creepy convents and even Maria Monk! There are certain Catholic practices, too, that they disagree with, which are shared by many Protestant denominations.

CHAPTER 26

BIRTHDAYS, CHRISTMAS AND EASTER

The Watchtower forbids its followers from observing birthdays, Easter and Christmas, and of course it condemns the Catholic celebration of saint's days. Its justification for forbidding birthday celebrations is that in the Bible, when birthdays are mentioned, something bad always happens: Pharaoh hangs his baker at his birthday (Genesis 40:20-22) and John the Baptist was beheaded during Herod's birthday (Matthew 14: 6-10). Therefore, birthdays are a bad thing and are part of paganism.

Needless to say, we don't celebrate birthdays because they are of pagan origin and the Biblical references do not amount to a Scriptural prohibition. Let us just celebrate the uniqueness of every human being by celebrating their birthday and enjoy the fact that our God is the God of life.

What is the Catholic response to the Watchtower disapproval of our celebrations?

When was Christmas?

The Watchtower is probably correct when it says that Jesus was not born on 25th December. It is, however, incorrect to say that the Church decided to celebrate the birth of Jesus on that day to take it over from the pagan celebration of Saturnalia and the feast of Sol Invictus, the unconquered Sun, of the Mithraic religion. (Actually, the Feast of Sol Invictus occurred a week later, with the week of Saturnalia leading up to it). There is no mention at all in the literature of the early Church that says this was the reason.

The most likely time of the year for Jesus' birth is September. The most likely explanation is the calculation from the priestly division of Abijah mentioned in Luke 1:5. The order for when the priestly families performed their duties is given in 1 Chronicles 24:7-18. The course of Abijah was eighth and the cycle began on the first Sabbath of Nisan. Each family, 24 in all, served for one week twice a year, excluding the feasts of Passover, Pentecost and Tabernacles, when all would be required to attend. Zechariah, then, would have served during Sivan, around June, and Kislev, six months later.

If June is taken as the most likely month of service, then John the Baptist would have been born in the Spring, around the Feast of Passover. It is interesting that during the Passover celebration Jewish families leave an empty place and an extra cup of wine for Elijah the prophet, and the wife of the family goes out to the door to look for him, for Jewish tradition expected Elijah to return at Passover. Jesus said that he did return in the person of John the Baptist (though not as a reincarnation!).

Since Jesus was conceived six months after John that means he was born in September. This is appropriate, given the Jewish feasts around that time. Mid September is the

Feast of Succot, or Tabernacles, when the Jewish people erect a booth in their gardens and live in it for seven days, commemorating their sojourn in the wilderness after escaping from Egypt. Was John alluding to this when he said that 'the Word was made flesh and dwelt among us' (John 1:14) literally, 'pitched his tent among us'? Succot is also known as 'the Season of our Joy', and the 'Feast of the Nations'. Is there a hint of this in the angels' greeting to the shepherds, 'Fear not, for I bring you tidings of great joy, which shall be to all people', the traditional greeting for the Feast of Succot? In addition, as the celebrants enter the booth or Succah, there is the ceremony of Ushpizin, welcoming the *shekinah*, or God's presence, with seven faithful shepherds of Israel. Again, September and October are the last months when it would be feasible to be outdoors at night, as the shepherds were; the weather can be mild in December, though, so this would not absolutely rule out a December date.

Another tradition is that Jesus died on the date of his birthday, which would fix it in the Spring[26].

But there are reasons for 25th December being set as the date of Jesus' birth. St Cyril of Alexandria (348-386), saw the census documents ordered by Caesar Augustus, which gave the date as 25th December, although these census records are no longer extant.

There is also another method of reckoning the date working backwards from the destruction of the Temple of Jerusalem in A.D 70, when the course of Jehoiarib was serving. If there was no break in service, then the course of Abijah was serving in the first week of October. St John

---

[26] It is possible that there was a confusion concerning the understanding of the Incarnation of Jesus, which of course took place at his conception and which we celebrate on the 25th March, Feast of the Annunciation.

Chrysostom (347-407), taught that Zechariah received his vision on the Day of Atonement, which falls in September or October. This would place John the Baptist's birth in June or July and Jesus' birth in December or January, which fits in with the traditional dates of the Catholic celebration of 25th December and also the Eastern Orthodox celebration on 6th January. As early as 221 A.D. Julius Africanus was recording the date of Jesus' birth as 25th December, as well as St Hippolytus, around the same time.

It really does not matter which day was Jesus' birth, because one thing we do know is that he was born! I pointed out that when we celebrate Jesus' birth on 25th December we are celebrating a liturgical day, not necessarily the exact date of his birth, but of course the Witnesses refused to accept that, because they do not have any liturgical celebrations. We do not know if the Transfiguration took place on the 6th August, for example, or that Mary's birthday was on the 8th September, but it is good that we remember, recall, the events of Jesus' life, of those of Mary and the saints, just as we have family celebrations. Most saints' days are celebrated on the day of their death: that is, the day of their birth into heaven. We are part of that great family of Jesus and his saints, and so we celebrate these birthdays. The Watchtower condemns all such commemorations of the incidents of Jesus' life and of his saints.

Easter

The Watchtower also forbids the celebration of Easter, because it attributes the name Easter as deriving from the goddess Astarte, and says that the celebrations connected with Easter, such as hot cross buns and dyed eggs, originated in Chaldean rites, (*Reasoning from the Scriptures,* pp. 179, 180), quoting from a book by Alexander Hislop. Eggs were indeed used in pagan fertility rites, but for Christians they are a symbol of new life; since eggs are part of God's creation, then of course they can be used by Christians as symbols of their faith. Hot cross buns are signed with a cross to remind us of the crucifixion, and the buns are made up of only ingredients that were permitted during Lent.

It is very unlikely that Hislop was correct in attributing the word Easter to Astarte. Saint Bede the Venerable derived it from Eastre, the goddess of Spring.

Of course, the celebration of Easter has nothing at all to do with any pagan cult but with the Resurrection of Jesus Christ. It is possible that St Paul is referring to the earliest Christian celebration of Christ's Resurrection in 1 Corinthians 5:7, 8: 'Clear out the old yeast, so that you may become a fresh batch of dough, inasmuch as you are unleavened. For our paschal lamb, Christ, has been sacrificed. Therefore let us celebrate the feast, not with the old yeast, the yeast of malice and wickedness, but with the unleavened bread of sincerity and truth.' Since the death and resurrection of Christ had superseded the Passover, then this is most probably an indication that the Christians were now gathering to celebrate their new Passover instead, just as the Christian Eucharist was superseding the Sabbath celebrations (cf. Acts 20:7-12).

CHAPTER 27

CELEBRATING MARY AND THE SAINTS

Mary, Mother of the Lord

The Watchtower is generous in its appreciation of Mary, in her willingness to listen to God, her courage to act in harmony with his will and to be used by him, her purity and her prayer (see *Reasoning From the Scriptures,* pp. 254-255). They acknowledge that she was a virgin at Jesus' conception, but do not believe that she remained a virgin.

They make the point that in Matthew 13:53-56 the people talk of Jesus' 'brothers' as James, Joseph, Simon and Jude, as well as his sisters. However, the Church has always seen these as his cousins, since there was no word for cousin in Hebrew or Aramaic, and the term 'brother' covered a whole range of relationships, including that of Jesus' disciples.

It quotes from *The New Catholic Encyclopaedia 1967* as saying that in the Greek *adelphos* 'would naturally be taken by his Greek reader' as referring to full blood brother and sister. However, the online version makes no reference to this so I can't verify this.[27] The online version identifies James 'the brother of the Lord' with James, son of Alpheus since the other James, son of Zebedee, was dead by the time mentioned in Acts 15:6ff and Galatians 2:9-12 when St Paul saw 'the brother of the Lord.

Comparing John 19:25 with Matthew 27:56 and Mark 15:40, Mary wife of Clophas, Mary's sister or sister-in-law, is the mother of James (the Less) as well as Joseph or Joses. Moreover, the names of her sons and the order in which they are given, no doubt, the order of seniority, warrant us in identifying these sons with James and Joseph, or Joses, the "brethren" of the Lord. The existence among the early followers of Christ of two sets of brothers having the same names in the order of age, is not likely.

There are other indications in the Gospels that Jesus was the only son of Mary and Joseph. Mary is always identified as the mother of Jesus, but of no other sons or daughters. Luke 2:41-50 recounts the incident when the family went to Jerusalem for the Feast of the Passover 'as usual'. If Mary had had four other sons as well as daughters after the birth of Jesus to when he was twelve years old, it is most unlikely she would have been able to make the long journey. Besides, it mentions only Jesus as being with Mary and Joseph. Finding Jesus missing they went to find him among their friends and relations, surely among his cousins.

At the foot of the Cross, (John 19:26-27), Jesus gives his mother into the care of John the Beloved Disciple; this would have been highly insulting and unnecessary if Mary had had other sons and daughters whose responsibility it would have been to look after her.

---

[27] See the article under 'Brethren of the Lord'.

Mary, sinless Mother of God, assumed into heaven

The Watchtower believes Mary was neither sinless, nor the Mother of God. It quotes Luke 2:22-24 'When the day came for them to be purified'. She, too, it concludes, 'had inherited sin and imperfection from Adam' (*Reasoning From the Scriptures,* p. 258). It here muddles ritual 'uncleanness' with personal sin and is further implying that the act of giving birth is sinful!

The offering was made for both Jesus and Mary: 'When the day came for *them*'.... If the Watchtower believes it meant Mary was not sinless, then it would have to apply that reasoning to Jesus as well.

Mary is truly the Mother of God; not that she gave birth to Jesus' divine nature but to her unique Son, a Person indivisible, who is both God and Man.

> Now a great sign appeared in heaven; a woman adorned with the sun, standing on the moon, and with the twelve stars on her head for a crown (Revelation 12:1).

Some commentaries (eg. JB), see this vision as referring to Israel as the mother of the messianic saviour, but since Mary had been living under John's care the Church has always seen it as referring also to Mary, the archetype of the Church.

Reverence and love for Mary

'Reasoning From the Scriptures' p. 260 speaks of 'the adoration of Mary', but of course Catholics and the Orthodox do not worship her but give her great reverence as being the Mother of the Lord, and also our Mother,

because she has always seen that when Jesus gave Mary into the care of John and Mary was given to the disciple, that she has been given to us as our mother, too. Jesus gives her the title of 'woman' (cf. John 2:3, 4; 19:26-27), not a term of denigration but a term of respect, speaking also of her position as the 'new Eve', reversing the shame of the First Woman, Eve.

In Luke 11:27, 28, a woman cries out 'Happy the womb that bore you and the breasts you sucked!' But he replied, 'Still happier those who hear the word of God and keep it!' Jesus is not denigrating his mother here, but pointing to the fact that her faith, her hearing the word of God and pondering it in her heart, (Luke 2:51), believing it and acting on it, is of even greater import than giving birth to him in the flesh. Her example of faith is given to us as the model of our response to God's will.

The Saints

If Mary has a very special place in the hearts of Catholics, the saints, our brothers and sisters in the faith, are also honoured. The celebration of saint's days began very early on, but it was the day of their birthday into heaven that was celebrated. It was customary for the Christians to gather and celebrate Mass over the tomb of a martyr on the day of his birth into heaven. We belong to a family, the family of God, and just as we celebrate the birthdays of those nearest and dearest to us, of our family and friends, so also we remember our brothers and sisters in the faith who have gone before us. It reminds us of the unbroken chain of faith that goes right back to the beginning of the Church at Pentecost. As we remember them year by year it is very encouraging to remind ourselves of that great cloud of witnesses, (Hebrews 12:1), to remember their lives and to be aware once again that holiness occurs everywhere and anywhere and that we can strive for it, too.

Most Catholics have their favourite saint, to whom they turn and ask for their prayers. There are also great saints of the Church who have left us their writings on the faith and on the spiritual life, so not only their example but also their wisdom helps us on our own journey to God. We can be confident of the power of their prayer. Just as we turn to our friends and ask for their prayer, so we turn to our brothers and sisters in the faith who are now with God; being in the full vision before the face of God, they know completely God's will for us and how that may best be accomplished in our lives and so can help us on our journey to God.

It reminds us that even in the darkest days of the Church there were always outstanding Christians who gave their lives for Christ, who gave light and vision to their fellow Christians by the radiance of their lives. And now, in our own time, we have even more martyrs bearing witness to their faith. It encourages us to strive to do likewise.

Statues and Pictures

We have holy pictures and also statues as pictorial reminders of them, just as we have photos of friends and family. In their books and pamphlets The Watchtower also have pictures of Jesus and God the Father, as well as the paradise earth as they picture it. We do not break the 2nd Commandment, 'you shall not make yourself a carved image or any likeness of anything in heaven or on earth beneath or in the waters under the earth; you shall not bow down to them or serve them' (Exodus 20:4, 5). With Jesus taking on flesh so that whoever saw him saw the Father, the Church saw that we can now picture the holy things, the holy ones of God.

We do not worship our statues of Jesus, Mary and, the saints, but they remind us of them. We are body and soul, and the Church has always recognised our need for tangible things to remind us of God and the things of God. Ours is a sacramental faith, where grace, the life of God, is given to us through tangible things, bread and wine, water, oil, breath – and art.

The Rosary

The Rosary has almost become a symbol of a Catholic! The objection that the Watchtower and many Protestants have about this form of prayer is that it seems to go against what Jesus said in Mathew 6:7: 'In your prayers do not babble as the pagans do, for they think that by using many words they will make themselves heard'. Our prayer to our heavenly Father is not like that, nor is the rosary. There is no Scriptural objection to repetition in prayer; Jesus himself repeated the same prayer in the Garden of Gethsemane (cf. Matthew 26:45), and many of the psalms are repetitious (cf. Psalm 136). Jesus himself urged us to be insistent in our prayer (cf. Luke 18:1), an insistence that is not from fear of an unhearing god, but from perseverance and trust, in sheer joy and thanksgiving; the rosary, which is steeped in Scripture, is a wonderful aid to meditation and contemplation of the life of Jesus, especially through the eyes and the prayer of Mary, and a powerful prayer of intercession.

CHAPTER 28

THE POPE AND PRIESTS

The Watchtower, of course, does not accept the primacy of the Pope. In commenting on the passage of Matthew 16:13-19, on which the mandate is given to Simon bar Jonah, renamed Peter, the Rock, to express his new role in the Church Jesus founds on him, the Watchtower rightly points out (*Reasoning From the Scriptures,* pp. 37, 38) that Jesus is called the Rock and the cornerstone, making the assumption that therefore Peter cannot be the Rock as well. However, it is precisely because Jesus is the Rock and the cornerstone that Jesus has the authority to bestow it also upon Peter, to act in his name and with his authority (Matthew 28:18,19).

Throughout the New Testament Peter is always mentioned first – it is Peter, James and John, for example - and Jesus gives to him the keys of the Kingdom of heaven to bind and to loose. To understand the import of this we need to read Isaiah 22:20-22, where Eliakim the son of Hilkiah is given the keys of the kingdom as Chamberlain to the king and given the authority to act in his name, which is the same position Jesus gives to Peter.

Since Jesus has promised to be with his Church until the end of time, then the office of Peter will continue in the Church until the Lord comes again. Although Peter was the first bishop of Rome (1 Peter 5:13 shows that Peter was in Rome, because Babylon was the code name for Rome), from the very beginning the primacy of Peter was seen to extend to other communities, and to be handed on:

> The blessed apostles, then, having founded and built up the Church, committed into the hands of Linus the office of the episcopate. Of this Linus, Paul makes mention in the Epistles to Timothy. To him succeeded Anacletus; and after him, in the third place from the apostles, Clement was allotted the bishopric. This man, as he had seen the blessed apostles, and had been conversant with them, might be said to have the preaching of the apostles still echoing [in his ears], and their traditions before his eyes. Nor was he alone [in this], for there were many still remaining who had received instructions from the apostles. In the time of this Clement, no small dissension having occurred among the brethren at Corinth, the Church in Rome despatched a most powerful letter to the Corinthians, exhorting them to peace, renewing their faith, and declaring the

tradition which it had lately received from
the apostles.[28]

This is an important extract in showing how the faith was passed down in the early years of the Church. Contrary to what the Watchtower asserts, there was no break in continuity with the apostles and the teaching they handed down to the Christians. Even to the third generation of the bishops of Rome they were men who had received the faith from the lips of the apostles themselves; they had seen that faith in action and in tradition that was just as important and valid as the spoken word. This was before the writings that would form the New Testament had been widely circulated and perhaps even written.

Clement, the third bishop of Rome and therefore Pope, wrote to the Christians in Corinth, although they had a bishop of their own, to settle a dispute. There was therefore the assumption that the Pope's authority extended beyond his own diocese of Rome, and that this was taken for granted and accepted that he had this Church -wide jurisdiction.

Priestly abuse

One of the most serious of the issues concerning the Church, and headlined in the media, is priestly sexual abuse. At one meeting with the Witnesses she brought this issue up, and since I had heard of some incident that concerned a

---

[28] St Irenaeus, *Against the Heresies,* Book 3, Chapter 3. Quoted in John R. Willis S.J, *The Teachings of the Church Fathers,* (New York, Ignatius Press 2002), pp. 72, 73. This volume, as well as Patrick Madrid, *Why is That in Tradition?* (Huntingdon, Our Sunday Visitor, 2002), gives excellent extracts from the Church Fathers on the teachings of the Church.

Jehovah's Witness, I mentioned this. The Witness blushed, lowered her head and muttered that all organisations have problems. I agreed with her, and pointed out that I would not have brought up the matter of wrong-doing in her own organisation if she had not done so first about the Church. If you wish to explore this problem in the Watchtower, there is a website – *silentlambs.org*.

However, I never bring this issue up with a Witness myself, or any other moral failings of the Watchtower Organisation, unless they themselves initiated it, because, as the Witness acknowledged, there are failings in every organisation. Incidentally, as I pointed out to her, statistically there is far less abuse in the Catholic Church than in any other part of society.

Since clerical abuse hit the headlines there have been even more cases of sexual abuse in secular organisations and individuals, which puts the abuse in the Church in perspective. However, we can never minimise the effect it has had on the victims of such abuse, especially when it comes from people who should be above reproach; we should pray for the victims, but also for those wrongly accused, whose lives will have been ripped apart. Should we not also pray for the abusers that the grace of God will penetrate their hearts, too, because God wants all to be saved and come to knowledge of the truth.

CONCLUSION

My concern is with the teachings and doctrines of the Watchtower Organisation, which I feel, strongly, is depriving thousands of people of the full life in Christ that Jesus offers to everyone. I am hoping that this book will give my fellow Catholics, especially, the knowledge that will enable them to counter the arguments put forward by the Watchtower.

Yes, our Church is not perfect, because it is made up of imperfect human beings, but it is also adorned with outstanding examples of the fullness of Christian living in the saints and of the holy people we ourselves might know. All that Jesus has given us to live that full Christian life is there in the Catholic Church, regardless of the frailty of its individual members.

My prayer is that what I have written will be of help to one who may be wavering in their faith, to open their eyes to the beauty of the Catholic Church and to a deeper commitment to living out their faith within that Church, our Mother.

APPENDIX 1

And when we say also that the Word, who is the first-birth of God, was produced without sexual union, and that He, Jesus Christ, our Teacher, was crucified and died, and rose again, and ascended into heaven, we propound nothing different from what you believe regarding those whom you esteem sons of Jupiter. For you know how many sons your esteemed writers ascribed to Jupiter: Mercury, the interpreting word and teacher of all; Aesculapius, who, though he was a great physician, was struck by a thunderbolt, and so ascended to heaven; and Bacchus too, after he had been torn limb from limb; and Hercules, when he had committed himself to the flames to escape his toils; and the sons of Leda, and Dioscuri; and Perseus, son of Danae; and Bellerophon, who, though sprung from mortals, rose to heaven on the horse Pegasus. For what shall I say of Ariadne, and those who, like her, have been declared to be set among the stars? And what of the emperors who die among yourselves, whom you deem worthy of deification, and in whose behalf you produce some one who swears he has seen the burning Caesar rise to heaven from the funeral pyre? And what kind of deeds are recorded of each of these reputed sons of Jupiter, it is needless to tell to those who already know. This only shall be said, that they are written for the advantage and encouragement of youthful scholars; for all reckon it an honourable thing to imitate the gods.

But far be such a thought concerning the gods from every well-conditioned soul, as to believe that Jupiter himself, the governor and creator of all things, was both a parricide and the son of a parricide, and that being overcome by the love of base and shameful pleasures, he came in to Ganymede and those many women whom he had violated and that his sons did like actions. But, as we said above, wicked devils perpetrated these things. And we have learned that those only are deified who have lived near to God in holiness and virtue; and we believe that those who live wickedly and do not repent are punished in everlasting fire.

Moreover, the Son of God called Jesus, even if only a man by ordinary generation, yet, on account of His wisdom, is worthy to be called the Son of God; for all writers call God the Father of men and gods. And if we assert that the Word of God was born of God in a peculiar manner, different from ordinary generation, let this, as said above, be no extraordinary thing to you, who say that Mercury is the angelic word of God. But if any one objects that He was crucified, in this also He is on a par with those reputed sons of Jupiter of yours, who suffered as we have now enumerated. For their sufferings at death are recorded to have been not all alike, but diverse; so that not even by the peculiarity of His sufferings does He seem to be inferior to them; but, on the contrary, as we promised in the preceding part of this discourse, we will now prove Him superior--or rather have already proved Him to be so--for the superior is revealed by His actions. And if we even affirm that He was born of a virgin, accept this in common with what you accept of Ferseus. And in that we say that He made whole the lame, the paralytic, and those born blind, we seem to say what is very similar to the deeds said to have been done by Aesculapius.

Justin Martyr

APPENDIX 2

This extract comes from the book The Jehovah's Witnesses by Friedrich Wilhelm Haak, revised in 1997. The book is written in German and Brian Gale has translated the following letter extract.

Dear Reich Chancellor,

On the 25th June 1933 at the sports hall Wilmersdorf, Berlin, a conference was convened by some 5000 delegates of the Bible Students of Germany (JWs), representing several millions of Germans. These have for many years been friends and supporters of this movement. The purpose of this convention was for these representatives to explore ways, to inform the Reich Chancellor and the other esteemed officials of the German Empire, as well as to all other states the following standpoints:

In certain parts of the country measures have been and are being taken against Christian men and women, who are unified in their positive belief. This in essence amounts to the persecution of Christians by other Christians, in that there have been accusations against us from the clerical front (especially from the Catholics) and which are untrue.

Though we are absolutely convinced of the objectivity of government departments and individual officials, we nevertheless observe, because of the extent of our literature and demands of the examiners of the material, the content and significance of our organisation is generally being falsely judged, and also is what our religious opponents in full prejudice bring against us.

Therefore, Mr Reich Chancellor, the conference agreement with its accompanying explanation, is laid before you (and the leaders of the German Reich) by the Watchtower Bible and Tract Society, so that you may accept it as documentation of the fact that the Bible Students of Germany have but one single goal in their work; they purposely lead people back to God, to witness to and honour the name of Jehovah the Almighty, the father of our lord and saviour Jesus Christ. We know for certain that you, Mr Reich Chancellor, will not allow such activity to be disturbed.

The Bible Student community and their associates are universally known as being a bastion of true reverence for the Almighty and are zealous guardians of careful biblical research. Local police authorities would have to agree, the Bible Students must count as belonging to those elements in the country and amongst the people who have a great love of order. Their sole mission is to gather human hearts for God.

The Watchtower Bible and Tract Society is the organising mission control body of the Bible Students – for Germany, H.Q. is Magdeburg.

The Brooklyn presidium of the Watchtower has always from the outset been German friendly. As a result of this in 1918 the president of the Society and the seven members of the governing body in America were sentenced to eighty years in jail, because the president refused to use two magazines to incite war propaganda against Germany. These two journals 'Watchtower' and 'Bible Student' were the only ones in the entire country which rejected the pressure for war propaganda, and were therefore banned and repressed in America.

In the same way our Society's presidium not only refused to take part in recent months, in the horror stories against Germany, but has even taken an opposing stand, which is underlined in the accompanying explanation; the clue to this is that the elements leading this onslaught of war propaganda (horror stories) in America, i.e., the Jews with business interests and Catholics, are also the ones who are conducting the most rigorous persecution against this Society and its leadership. By this and other resolutions hereby given, the rejection of this insidious calumny should follow automatically, i.e. that the Bible Students were actually supported by the Jews. The five thousand delegates at their convention have with great satisfaction taken note of the ensuing statement by the local government president at Magdeburg, namely that the relationship between Bible Students and communists and Marxists, as maintained by our clerical opponents, is not provable (demonstrable), and is, therefore, also slanderous (libellous). A directly related press release was reported in the Madgeburg Daily News Nr 1 04 5th May 1933.

The conference of 5,000 delegates emphasised that, because of this state of affairs, they considered it beneath their dignity to have to defend themselves further against the despicable suspicion of indulging in communist or Marxist activity. These refuted libels by our religious opponents clearly bear the mark of religious rivalry, who instead of the honest rebuke and God's Word, would rather snuff out the truth with slander and libel.

Furthermore it was established by the 5,000 delegates, as expressed in the declaration, that the Bible Students of Germany are striving for the same high goals and ideals, as proclaimed by the government of the German Reich, regarding the relationship of man to God, namely (i.e.) the honesty (sincerity) of His creation, in response to the creator.

It was also established at the convention, that with reference to the relationship of the Bible Students to the National government (of the German Reich), no conflicts or differences of any kind exist, but on the contrary one can say – regarding the purely religious, unpolitical goals and efforts, - that these are in complete agreement with the parallel aims of the national government of the German Empire.

There has been a complaint against the alleged strong language in our literature, resulting in some banning of our books.

The conference of 5,000 delegates pointed in addition to the fact that the content of the books causing complaint related solely to circumstances and events in the Anglo-American world, and to Britain especially, which has been responsible for the League of Nations and the placing of unjust treaties and obligations upon Germany. In the above sense the statements of our literature, whether it be in respect to finance, politics or the papacy, are against the oppressors of the German land and people, yet certainly not against a Germany struggling under this burden, thus making the resulting ban fully incomprehensible.

For the German states in which even bans on our services and prayer meeting are in place, and those who have been waiting many weeks for a just solution to the gagging of their religious life, the following points are expressed:

We intend to go on complying with the imposed restrictions, since we are certain the Reich Chancellor, as well as the other states governments, will, in recognition of the real situation, lift these measures, by which tens of thousands of Christian men and women would have ultimately to perish as martyrs, akin to the early Christians.

Finally this conference of 5,000 delegates has declared, that the Bible Students or the Watchtower organisation represents a platform for the maintenance of order and security of the state (country), in addition to the demand of the national government for its own (aforementioned) high ideals on the religious front.

Above all in order that the Reich Chancellor, as leader of the people and all the other government leaders of the German Reich, and the German States, should be advised, this statement has been set out before you in some detail. This enclosed explanatory statement was read out by the secretary of the Bible Students convention (5,000 delegates) and unanimously accepted and approved by the latter, instructing them to hand over one copy of this declaration, together with the convention report to the Reich Chancellor and to each of the appropriate ministers of the German Empire and its state governments.

Following on from this most earnest application and explanation comes a humble plea, namely to grant an opportunity for a commission (delegation) from our number to present personally to the Reich Chancellor or Minister of the Interior (Home Office) a responsible and true representation of our situation. On the other hand the Reich Chancellor himself could appoint a commission, which is not opposed to us by religious prejudice and themselves would not be professionally religiously biased, but would evaluate our position totally without prejudice, corresponding to the Reich Chancellor's own just principles laid down for such purposes. With these principles in mind we beg to quote from point 24 of the manifesto of the German National Socialist Workers party: - "We demand the freedom for all religious persuasions within the state, in so far as they do not endanger its position, or offend against the moral and ethical sensibilities of the Germanic race. The party as such supports the view of a positive Christianity, without preference to any one denomination; it combats the spirit of Jewish materialism within and without, and is convinced that a lasting recovery of our people can only succeed from the inside out".

We too are firmly convinced that, if we are judged without religious prejudice, firstly according to God's word, secondly to the points set out in this application (petition), then the national German government will have no cause to prevent our services or missionary activity.

In anticipation of an expeditious and favourable consent, and the assurance of our utmost respect (high regard), we are, most honoured Reich Chancellor,

> Your most humble servants
> Watchtower Bible and Tract Society
> Magdeburg

Haak goes on to say:
They represent themselves as being victims of the Hitler dictatorship, making out they were singled out as being amongst the first, and therefore amongst the most important sufferers. It is true that many died in camps.

It is also true that Hitler received from Rutherford on 15th June (i.e. 10 days before the J.W. convention in Magdeburg), an obsequious address, emphasising his complete agreement with the parallel goals of the national government of the German Reich. Also included were:

1. Refusal to take part in war propaganda
2. Stand against business Jews and Catholics
3. Identification of the above people as being the most rigorous persecutors.

When the N.S. leaders clearly showed no interest in the aspirations of the American 'sect-firm', their supporters everywhere were called to send letters of protest to the N.S. The result is that the "Serious Bible Students" were rounded up and died in the camps. Not, however, for the leader of the German branch of the Society, Erich Frost. He it was who betrayed his Bible Student charges and their meeting places. In contrast to the wretched fate of the ordinary small 'publishers', he survived the Third Reich relatively unscathed, only to be re-established in office as a freedom fighter in 1945.

Reproduced in www.randytv.com/Hitler/germancomm.htm

BIBLIOGRAPHY

Catechism of the Catholic Church, London, Geoffrey Chapman, 1994.

D'Angelo, Louise, *The Catholic Answer to the Jehovah's Witnesses,* Meriden, Connecticut, The Maryheart Crusaders Inc.1981.

Finnerty, Robert, *Jehovah's Witnesses on Trial,* New Jersey, P&R Publishing 1993.

Franz, Raymond, *Crisis of Conscience,* Atlanta, Commentary Press 2004.

Gruss, Edmond (ed.), *We Left Jehovah's Witnesses*, New Jersey P&R Publishing 1974.

Harrison Barbara, *Visions of Glory*, New York, Simon & Schuster 1978.

Hoekema, A.A. *Jehovah's Witnesses*, Grand Rapids, Michigan, Paternoster Press 1973.

Holden, Andrew, *Jehovah's Witnesses,* USA & London, Routledge, 2002.

Horn, Trent, *20 Answers, Jehovah's Witnesses*, London, CTS, 2015.

James, Anthony, *Knock Knock, Who's There? The Truth About the Jehovah's Witnesses,* www.knockknockbook.co.uk.

Madrid, Patrick, *Answer Me This!* USA, Our Sunday Visitor, 2003.

Madrid, Patrick, *Why is That in Tradition?* USA, Our Sunday Visitor, 2002.

Morey, Robert, *How to Answer a Jehovah's Witness*, Minneapolis, Bethany House Publishers, 1980.

Schnell, William, *30 Years a Watchtower Slave*, USA, Baker Book House 1971.

Michael Sheehan, *Apologetics and Catholic Doctrine*, London, The Saint Austin Press, 2001.

Stevenson, W.C., *The Inside Story of Jehovah's Witnesses*, USA, Hart Publishing Co. 1967.

Thomas P.C., *General Councils of the Church*, USA, St Pauls Publications, 1993.

Tomsett, Valerie, *Released From the Watchtower*, London, Lakeland 1971.

Willis John R. S.J., *The Teachings of the Church Fathers*, New York, Ignatius Press, 2002.

Willis, Trevor, *Can Jehovah's Witnesses Survive?*, Kindle Edition 2013.

Watchtower Publications

Good News to Make You Happy 1976
Knowledge That Leads to Everlasting Life 1995
Let God be True 1946
Let Your Kingdom Come 1981
New World Translation of the Holy Scriptures 1961
Reasoning From the Scriptures 1985
Salvation 1939 (J.F Rutherford)
The Truth That Leads to Eternal Life 1968
What does the Bible Really Teach? 2005
You Can Live Forever in Paradise on Earth 1982

www.ingramcontent.com/pod-product-compliance
Lightning Source LLC
LaVergne TN
LVHW061541070526
838199LV00077B/6859